A

£3-

D1355829

John Butler Yeats

THE IRISH WRITERS SERIES
James F. Carens, General Editor

GEORGE FITZMAURICE	Arthur E. McGuinness
FRANCIS STUART	J. H. Natterstad
PATRICK KAVANAGH	Darcy O'Brien
WILLIAM ALLINGHAM	Alan Warner
SIR SAMUEL FERGUSON	Malcolm Brown
LADY GREGORY	Hazard Adams
GEORGE RUSSELL (AE)	Richard M. Kain and James O'Brien
THOMAS DAVIS	Eileen Sullivan
PEADAR O'DONNELL	Grattan Freyer
OLIVER ST. JOHN GOGARTY	J. B. Lyons
SEUMAS HEANEY	Robert Buttel

JOHN BUTLER YEATS

Douglas N. Archibald

821·912 YEA

~~851~~/YEA | 2 MAR 1979 129 T

LEICESTERSHIRE LIBRARIES
AND INFORMATION SERVICE

Lewisburg
BUCKNELL UNIVERSITY PRESS

London: Associated University Presses

DO NOT LOTIFY STSS

© 1974 by Associated University Presses, Inc.

Associated University Presses, Inc.
Cranbury, New Jersey 08512

Associated University Presses
108 New Bond Street
London W1Y OQX, England

Library of Congress Cataloging in Publication Data

Archibald, Douglas N
    John Butler Yeats.

    (The Irish writers series)
    Bibliography: p.
    1. Yeats, John Butler, 1839–1922—Biography.
PR5899.Y6Z62   821¹.8–[B]   71–125792
ISBN 0–8387–7759–7
ISBN 0–8387–7733–3 (pbk.)

For my Father

A few score men such as your father
in the world at any one time
would cure its sickness. . . .

John Sloan to Elizabeth Yeats
February 7, 1922

PRINTED IN THE UNITED STATES OF AMERICA

DO NOT NOTIFY STSS

Contents

Preface

According to John Sloan and most other qualified observers, John Butler Yeats was a productive and talented but never quite successful painter. G. K. Chesterton said he was "perhaps the best talker I ever knew," and an acquaintance told W. B. Yeats that his father was "the greatest conversationalist in New York." He was a minor writer, producing over a dozen essays, several reviews, a fragment of an autobiography, two poems, and two stories and a play that have not been published. He was also an indefatigable correspondent, who wrote hundreds of letters (many still unpublished) to family and friends in Ireland, England, and America. He was a presence and a force in many significant lives—John Synge, George Russell (AE), Susan Mitchell, York Powell, Ezra Pound, John Sloan, Van Wyck Brooks, John Quinn, and others. History has identified him as the father of Ireland's foremost modern painter and the world's leading modern poet, a more or less gay antagonist in the Oedipal drama sketched by the biographers.

JBY (the initials are economical and conveniently distinguish him from his famous offspring) was also something his son William admired and envied and, because of his own historical location, never quite managed to be—the last Anglo-Irish gentleman. He was an inheritor of values, experiences, and attitudes that go back to the Plantations, the Ascendancy, and the Irish Parliament of 1782–1800, that were constricted during the nineteenth century and impossible during the twentieth. If his own buoyant intelligence, his young friends, and his children kept him in lively touch with modernism, his age and his ancestry reminded him that he shared much with Isaac Butt and Edward Dowden, Grattan and Emmet, Swift, Goldsmith, and Barrington as well.

Those are the controlling points of departure for this introduction to a life. That complex, intriguing, and generally misperceived topic—JBY's relationship with his elder son—has been for the most part excluded. It requires too much space, and it is probably best to have one study where the elder Yeats is allowed to stand on his own. Because the bulk of JBY's writing, including the letters, is unpublished, uncollected, out of print, or otherwise difficult to come by, I have summarized and quoted in an attempt to capture the flavor and the quality of his mind; and I have retained JBY's spelling, punctuation, and affection for italics. The quoted material is from his writings unless otherwise indicated. (For example: "JBY said to Sloan" refers to *John Sloan's New York Scene*, "JBY wrote Quinn" to B. L. Reid's *Quinn*.)

A reasonably complete bibliography follows. For Anglo-Irish matters I have depended most upon the Yeatses themselves and upon Joseph Hone and William M. Murphy. For JBY's life in New York I have drawn primarily from his letters and from the references and anecdotes of John Sloan, Van Wyck Brooks, and B.L. Reid. My friend and colleague Philip Marcus has read the manuscript, made suggestions, and taught me much about Irish life and letters. I am most grateful to the Colby College Library for providing me with a photograph of one of JBY's self-portraits, and to Senator Michael B. Yeats and Miss Ann Yeats for permission to quote from the various writings of their grandfather.

Chronology

1893   Born in Tullyish, County Down in eastern Ulster
1849   The Miss Davenport's School at Seaforth, near Liverpool
1851   The Athol Academy on the Isle of Man
1857   Trinity College, Dublin
1862   Father dies; inherits small property in Kildare
1863   Marries Susan Pollexfen of Sligo
1865   W. B. Yeats born; followed by Susan Mary ("Lily"), Elizabeth ("Lolly"), Robert, and Jack
1866   Called to the bar
1867   Heatherley's Art School in London
1869   The Academy School
1872   First Commissions
1873   Robert Yeats dies; begins education of W. B. Yeats
1880   Return to Dublin; cessation of rents from Kildare property
1887   Back to London
1900   Susan Yeats dies
1901   Family returns to Dublin
1908   To New York with Lily
1917   W.B. Yeats marries Georgie Hyde-Lees; Ann Butler born in 1919, Michael Butler in 1921

13

1918   Influenza and pneumonia; *Essays Irish and American*
1920   W. B. and Mrs. Yeats visit New York
1922   Dies in New York

John Butler Yeats

1

Anglo-Ireland

The Yeats ancestral background, like that of almost all the great Anglo-Irish families, is the middle-class world of shippers, merchants, rectors, and prudent marriages. Jervis Yeats, who died in 1712, probably came from Yorkshire and did establish a prosperous wholesale linen business in Dublin, which flourished under his son Benjamin. Family affairs seem to have declined under the second Benjamin Yeats, but he had married Mary Butler, who brought with her some 600 acres of land in Thomaston, County Kildare; she also brought—as it happened, more permanently—an attachment to one of the oldest and most illustrious Anglo-Irish families, the Earls of Ormond, and to a strain of Huguenot immigrants.

Their son, John Yeats (1774–1846), grandfather of JBY, won the Berkeley medal for Greek at Trinity College, Dublin, married Jane Taylor, daughter of a Dublin Castle official, took orders in the Church of Ireland, and, in 1805, was appointed to the living in Drumcliff, Sligo, where he remained for the rest of his life, and so established the family connection with the district. He left a reputation as a scholar and gentleman, as outdoorsman and entertainer, and as a Protestant rector who remained

on friendly and respecting terms with his Catholic
neighbors. His son, the first William Butler Yeats (1806–
62), went to TCD where he edited, with Isaac Butt, *The
Dublin University Review,* in which Carleton first published
his *Traits and Stories of the Irish Peasantry.* He too was an
athlete, enough of a horseman so that the rector of his
first parish complained that he thought he was being sent
a curate, but got a jockey instead. He was also a reader,
apparently of wide tastes.

William Yeats married Jane Grace Corbet; her grandfather had been a Registrar to the Lord Chancellor, her
brother was governor of Penang, and other relatives
had successful public or military careers. Years later he
was to retire to Sandymount Castle near Dublin—a large
eighteenth-century house with Gothic additions, extensive
grounds, and many memories—owned by Robert Corbet,
his wife's brother, a wealthy and hospitable man. JBY
spent many of his college days at Sandymount; in 1863
he brought his bride to "Georgeville," a new semi-
detached house close to the castle grounds. There William was born in 1865. Robert Corbert became one of
JBY's representative men, "a man of generous impulses . . . a gentleman, a worldling and a clubman . . . a
citizen of Dublin, of the type that flourished in the eighteenth century." He entertained interesting people and
collected paintings, and some of his nephew's devotion to
both probably stems from this period. Perhaps, too, Sandymount and its master are partly responsible for his idea
of the Georgian Anglo-Irish manner, its contented and
humorous acceptance of life, its charm and urbanity, its
courage and tolerance. Corbet's bankruptcy and suicide,
and the sale of the castle, contributed to JBY's decision

in 1867 to leave Dublin. He spoke frequently to his children of Sandymount and its owner, about how much he had grown and how contented he had been there, and the idea of life they represented became one of the poet's minor but sustained themes.

Soon after his marriage in 1835, the Reverend William Yeats was appointed rector to the large Ulster parish of Tullyish, County Down, where he officially regarded the Catholic Church as The Enemy, but never disliked its communicants as much as he did the dour and aggressive Presbyterians of the north. He was an eloquent preacher of evangelical tendencies, but his religion was never harsh or gloomy. In *Early Memories* (the fragment of autobiography that JBY never completed in spite of, or perhaps because of, much prodding), thinking of his father, JBY argues that in England eighteenth- and nineteenth-century evangelicalism influenced chiefly the middle class, making it more commercial by providing a religious view that accommodated the profit-and-loss ethic. But in Ireland it touched the never-mercantile small gentry, making them more tolerant and humane: "the wild men, described by Charles Lever, who cared for nothing except romance and courage and personal glory, now walked in the footsteps of their Lord and Master." The Reverend William Yeats did not restrict his ministry to the fortunate, and JBY remembers his working tirelessly to collect relief during the great famine, and fearlessly treating poor people during a cholera epidemic: "This was never forgotten to him in the parish. The poor have long memories."

It was a large and—*Early Memories* is persuasive—unusually happy family, "boisterous, full of animal spirits and health." JBY was older than his brothers and so often solitary and lonely, but he learned self-reliance and discovered "the world of fantasy . . . that land of endearing enchantment." He also became a companion to his father, from whom JBY learned that imagination and intellect—"make believe" and "honest thinking"— are not only compatible but complementary. JBY's remarkable gift of companionship and stimulation to his sons was partly his way of meeting a debt to his father, "who made me the artist I am, and kindled the sort of ambition I have transmitted to my sons."

The strength and sweetness of filial attachment is suggested by a dream JBY reported to his son in 1899, thirty-seven years after his father had died. It was a trying time for JBY—the letter is preoccupied with debts and difficulties—and the dream reveals anxieties about his improvidence, his children, and his trouble staying with a painting. But anxiety is cushioned, then displaced, by the dream's reanimation of love:

> Last night I had an amazing dream—I thought I was listening to a wonderful sermon by my father—he and I afterwards walked up and down an old garden and to all my delighted compliments he only answered "it was very loosely constructed." I remember constantly trying to get hold of the M. S. that I might see his handwriting, which I have not seen for many years and which I have always wanted to see—my father was a man who excited strong affection. Afterwards came a lot of events causing to me great pleasure. A sort of dissolving view in which joy succeeded joy. At the end when all the rest had dispersed I found written on an unnoticed piece of paper the words, "The apple tree has been made free"—and all seemed to be a consequence of my father's sermon. . . .

P.S. After the dream had departed I mused long on the words "the apple tree has been made free" being still in that state of semi-consciousness which treats a dream as a series of realities and came to the conclusion that it meant the apple tree that was in Eden; which seemed to me a very tremendous and beautiful revelation.

If early childhood was happy, school days were not. At the age of ten, as his father's initial attempts at formal education were no more promising than JBY's were to be with his own eldest son, he was sent to Miss Davenport's school at Seaforth, near Liverpool. It was very fashionable, proper, and British, directed in theory by a Sense of Duty, but actually by the Fear of Hell. From Seaforth he went to Athol Academy, a boys' school on the Isle of Man run by a flogging headmaster, which seems to have been an experience of unremitting gloom—"that Scotchman brushed the sun out of my sky." The unhappiness was interrupted by the delirious joy of the long summer holidays, which cemented close family feelings and made him more fully appreciate the gentleness and tolerance of his father's religion and the bright and warm quirkiness of his mind. Evangelical he was, and hell surely formed a part of his theology, but he never threatened or manipulated his children with that "dismal and absurd doctrine."

Like other children of the nineteenth century, JBY survived his early education and, in 1857, entered Trinity College, where he took a degree in classics, metaphysics, and logic and was interested, he recalls, in very little beyond the already familiar Greek, Latin, and Euclid: "I had been braced too tight, now I was braced too lightly: self-abandoned to a complete relaxation. . . .

I did not think, I did not work, I had no ambition, I
dreamed." He remembers TCD without great affection
or respect, though he did rather hope that Willie
would attend, and the University made its mark. It did
not train him professionally or shape him intellectually,
but it did provide friends, foster attitudes, and create
associations. JBY grew more fully aware and articulate
about what it meant, politically and culturally, to
be an Anglo-Irish Protestant and a gentleman. Though
Trinity paid little attention to the arts, it was, as Joseph
Hone said, "full of brilliant young men, figures thirty
years later in the last efflorescence of the Ireland of
Burke and Goldsmith." JBY's contemporaries (or near
contemporaries) included the scholars Mahaffy, Tyrell,
and Madden; the physicist George Fitzgerald; Thomas
Allingham, the poet's brother; future bishops and
judges and others destined for important positions in
Ireland and the Empire. Between 1857 and 1867 they
provided friendship, support, and standards to accept,
modify, or reject. They helped him to decide who he was
(which he came to know very well) and where he was
going (about which he was never altogether sure).

One of his closest friends from college until the end
of the century was Edward Dowden, famous scholar,
serious poet, and embodiment of Dublin's academic
culture. Twentieth-century readers aware of Dowden
probably know him through his scholarship, especially
the life of Shelley and the studies of Shakespeare, or
through the portrait in *Reveries over Childhood and Youth*. The
first is a limited acquaintance, the second unfair, more the
views of WBY in 1922 than of JBY many years earlier.
There is truth in the poet's account of his father's feelings,

but the language of failure, timidity, and provinciality, and the conclusion that their "friendship . . . had long been an antagonism" is misleading. JBY was never so patronizing or hostile. Their letters show real affection and respect. Dowden's reveal the wary regard of the scholar for the artist; he feels deeply about JBY, earnestly worries about his wayward ideas and casual profession; and he is careful about the sharp tongue and the firm though unsystematic opinions. The painter tests and rejuvenates him. JBY is amiable, amused, concerned; he takes Dowden seriously even when he is teasing. Nevertheless, later letters about the professor suggest that the figure of Dowden has become an emblem of the trap of established culture. He was, JBY feels, a natural poet blighted by TCD and its "great Protestant doctrine of getting on," by chilly Unionist politics, by a suppression of feeling for sensuous beauty, and by nineteenth-century science and materialism. He marked one of the ways it was better not to go.

There were other roads to travel that JBY did not then recognize. Standish O'Grady followed him at TCD by slightly less than a decade, or one student generation. Their situations were strikingly similar. Both men were the sons of Protestant clergymen and small landowners; both were expected to take orders but, too skeptical and independent, chose a career at law instead, which they both soon abandoned for art, culture, and scholarship. Neither had, at college, any sense of indigenous Irish history, but both had received a strenuous early education and both loved the wild and dark countryside of their childhoods—a combination that was to produce, in each, an inclination to combine

history and story, fact and legend, in their perception
of the Irish past. At about the time JBY was beginning
his career as a painter, O'Grady almost accidentally
discovered Sylvester O'Halloran and Eugene O'Curry,
and hence the body of Irish myth and history to which
he devoted the rest of his life. In some ways, JBY became
what O'Grady would have been without that discovery.
Both men saw that the Protestant landowning class
that produced them was moribund. O'Grady was
haunted by it, and later became bitter and strident as
he measured the distance between the old Celtic
aristocracy and the nineteenth-century landlords. JBY,
while aware of their insufficiency and irresponsibility,
remained more relaxed, even affectionate, trying to
mitigate the shame and articulate the accomplishments
of their shared past.

Another decisive figure during the 1850s and '60s
was his father's old friend, Isaac Butt, M.P., Q.C.,
Professor of Political Economy, and a definition of
nineteenth-century Anglo-Irish nationalism; he was once
a favorite of Disraeli and hope of the Irish Tories, then
magnanimous defender of imprisoned Fenians, finally
supplanted by Parnell as leader of the Home Rule
movement. JBY probably deviled for Butt in 1865–66,
when he was thinking of becoming a barrister, and
later did a magnificent chalk portrait. Butt seemed to
him a solitary and visionary uncomfortably caught
up in public life, a natural poet whose "poor Muse
could only visit him in strange places—in brothels and
gaming houses she met her son, himself an exile."
Once, when the world thought Butt was preparing for
a crucial public case, he went off alone to a country

inn and read *Paradise Lost*. He became one of JBY's figures of "naturalness and humanity" whose intellect and ambition were properly organized by his feelings, a persuasive rather than militant leader, "visibly enjoying the beliefs which he wants us to accept. . . . The cause he was fighting for enshrined itself in him—to follow him seemed health which is another name for happiness." Butt's career and its disasters also defined the fierce bitterness of Irish politics and JBY could never forgive Parnell for replacing his friend.

The lesson of Butt was to make JBY's nationalism critical rather than enthusiastic. Though a brave and loyal Irishman, and a Home-ruler, he never succumbed to blind political hatred; he never really embraced the Celtic Twilight; and he never hesitated to voice his reservations about political or cultural nationalism. A 1920 letter to his son concludes with this telling question: "I have just read Goethe's *Herman and Dorothea*—such a poem could not now be written, just as no one could write another Homer. And we see what is happening in Ireland. There also the actual has conquered and superseded the habitual. You discovered Ireland which had eluded Dowden and Todhunter, and now where is Ireland? and where are you?"

In one way—and it is probably the only way—his university years were typical of mid-nineteenth-century Great Britain: he lost his faith. When JBY read Butler's *Analogy*, he amazed himself by accepting the Bishop's premises but coming to exactly the opposite conclusion, "that revealed religion was myth and fable. . . . Everything now was gone, my mind a

contented negation. . . . I preferred sea & sky and
floating clouds to the finest pulpit oratory."

Orthodoxy gave way not to any of the available
doctrines, but to habits of mind: what Padriac Colum
later called his "serene and uncritical rationalism";
an amiable skepticism about the claims of organized
religion; a thorough and happy indifference to escha-
tologies; a generalized belief in a kind of higher utili-
tarianism, the greatest good understood imaginatively,
even whimsically, not materially. The nearest approx-
imation of an influence was John Stuart Mill, whose
works JBY now read and whose career he followed
when he went to London. It was the gentle, open,
and scrupulously honest Mill that JBY admired, and
he worried about the occasionally strident tone of his
own liberalism. Mill attracted him partly because he
recalled The Reverend William Yeats (it is easier to
reject a faith than a father, and JBY became something
of a genius at honoring men while differing with or
laughing at their opinions). Endorsing Mill, he had the
added pleasure of opposing Carlyle, a talky Englishman then the reigning sage of Dublin intellectual
circles; and Mill made it difficult to altogether dismiss
or hate England at the same time that he provided a
sound basis for judging British materialism, capitalism,
and imperialism.

JBY's most concrete debt to Mill was a £10 prize for
an essay in Political Economy (he was the only competitor),
his first earnings, which he used for a trip to Sligo
to visit ancestral country and his old friend from the
Athol Academy, George Pollexfen. The memory of
his arrival stayed with JBY for the rest of his life, and

in *Early Memories* and elsewhere he recalls it with
sustained pleasure and excitement: the strange, dark,
sea-battered beauty of the countryside; the Pollexfen
and Middleton families, so positive and so different;
"Dublin and my uneasy life there, and Trinity College,
though but a short day's journey, were obliterated,
and I was again with my school friend, the man
self-centered and tranquil and on that evening so
companionable."

His friend's father, William Pollexfen, descended
from Galway traders, ran away to sea as a boy, and
arrived in Sligo in 1833 to assist his cousin, Elizabeth
Middleton, whose husband had died during a cholera
epidemic. He married his cousin's daughter, also
Elizabeth, and joined her son, William Middleton,
in a prospering ship and mill business. He was the
very type of romantic and reckless Irishman that
fascinated JBY and delighted his son, the "silent and
fierce old man" that young William confused with God
and later associated with King Lear—indifferent to
popular opinion, yet respected, even loved; a strong
presence around whom legend easily grew. The
Middletons were not quite so vivid, but adventuresome
enough. William Middleton, Sr., had been a ship-owner
and smuggler working the route from London to
the Channel Islands and South America. His son was
apparently silent, ceremonious, conscientious, with
great self-discipline and personal authority. George
Pollexfen, the melancholy man and astrologer of WB's
poems and *Autobiographies,* was a bachelor and hypo-
chondriac, worked for the firm at Ballina, and seldom
visited Sligo except for race days. JBY was very

affectionate, admired his taciturn strength and instinctual wisdom; he also worried that George was trapped in duty and commerce—except for those rare and marvelous days when he was "mounted on a wild and splendid horse . . . a transformed being . . . then he loved all men, he loved humanity, he loved even himself."

In 1863, the year after his father died and JBY inherited the Kildare property and its income, he married Susan, the eldest, pretty, and much sought-after Pollexfen daughter. He later recalled that she accepted him because he was there a lot and the family helped. In many ways the marriage seems a representative, and melancholy, nineteenth-century arrangement: an active, buoyant husband and a passive, receding wife. Oliver Elton remembers Mrs. Yeats as "a silent, flitting figure . . . from the Fairy shores of Sligo," whose husband thought her "the right kind of mother for a poet and dreamer." Her health was poor: a cataract in one eye soon after marriage, a stroke in 1886 or '87 and another the following year from which she never recovered, living out her quiet life mostly in one room, feeding the birds at her window and never admitting that she was an invalid. The emotional burden of precarious finances fell largely on her; she was never really happy away from Sligo and spent as much time there as she could while her husband was in London or Dublin. She was not comfortable with artists and intellectuals and seems never to have gone to an exhibition of JBY's paintings or to have entered his studio. There was often real tension between them (JBY later said that he "would advise women not to marry either a poet or an artist. It is too dangerous, though like most dangerous things, it is enticing"). Neither her husband nor her children, who recall so much with such animation, say a great deal about her, and biographers have had to struggle for their portraits. Ten years after her death, JBY wrote two sympathetic and cheerful essays about American feminism, and it is difficult not to feel some uneasiness about his happy endorsement of lives and styles so different from those his wife was able to maintain.

Yet perhaps their uncharacteristic reticence is a kind of tribute. Jack Yeats said nothing about his mother's death in 1900, but his sketchbooks cease altogether for six months and do not return to their usual vigor and abundance until the following year. *Reveries* attests to the feelings for Sligo that she created in her children. The few times JBY does mention his wife, it is not only with affection, but with a sort of wondrous respect for the richness of her inner life, her natural kinship with the people of Sligo, and the sympathy behind her apparent reserve. Genial agnostic in so many matters, he steadfastly believes in the sanctity and permanence of marriage, and in the personal growth achieved through a solid one. When he was ill in New York in 1919, and again just before he died, he dreamed of her repeatedly.

Susan (indirectly) and George (explicitly) form the center of JBY's idea of the Pollexfens, his transformation of them from a family into an image and a lesson. "It is a curious fact," he recalls, "that entering this sombre house of stern preoccupation with business I for the first time in my life felt myself to be a free man." The stern and somber Pollexfens define his own freedom; but they have a force and presence that he lacks, envies, and—for the rest of his life—meditates upon. The two families become emblems for his mental and social universe, the terms of an unsystematic and shifting dialectic that shapes his perceptions. On the one hand, Yeatses, Dublin, the world and (later) Joyce; on the other, Pollexfens and Middletons, Sligo and Synge. His world values pleasure and growth; theirs order, duty, and direction. His occupies itself with ideas, opinions, and play; theirs is preoccupied by possessions, convictions, and industry. His thrives on art and intellect; theirs depends on nature and instinct. He sets a tone of gregarious amiability, they of silent and solitary strength. His characteristic accomplishment is one of range and intensity; theirs of depth and permanence. The one has to struggle to transcend a too-diffused identity; the other to escape from a too-narrow identity. JBY believes that his sons evolve from both worlds, but that the crucial strain in William comes from the critical and "eagerly communicative" Yeatses, in Jack from the instinctive Pollexfens. "Ah!" he remembers saying when he first realized that his son was a poet: "Behold I have given a tongue to the seacliffs."

So there is JBY in 1866, a young man with no settled career in view, but with a rich and various family and national history behind him. "As regards Ireland," he wrote in *Early Memories:*

our feelings were curious, and though exceedingly selfish not altogether so. We intended as good Protestants and Loyalists to keep the papists under our feet. We impoverished them, though we loved them, and their religion by its doctrine of submission and obedience unintentionally helped us, yet we were convinced that an Irishman, whether a Protestant or Catholic, was superior to every Englishman, that he was a better comrade and physically stronger and of greater courage.

It is a characteristic family attitude. There are expressions of it in the careers of the Reverend Yeatses of Drumcliffe and Tullyish; it appears throughout *Reveries over Childhood and Youth* and (in a different key) in Jack's *Sligo* and in the subject matter and feeling of many of his paintings. For JBY, his family, and others like them, there were actually four Irelands, and a man had to sort out his connections, commitments, and interpretations.

Growing up in Tullyish, JBY was surrounded by Ulster Presbyterians: northern Irishmen of Scots origin whom he found stiff and narrow in religion, embattled and determined in loyalty to England and in fearful contempt for Catholic nationalism, commercial in outlook and ethics. Going to college and working in Dublin, he encountered Irish Unionists, more relaxed and urbane than their northern counterparts, but still Anglicized in culture and politics—displaced Englishmen without the characteristic British virtues. JBY finally lumped together Ulstermen and Unionists in order to dismiss them. Whether angry or amused, he saw both as materialistic, Puritanical, and small-minded, colorless embodiments of "getting on," conventional receptacles of dogma and prejudice: "Protestantism makes a people energetic about *external* things and also arrogant and self-complacent, you know the Belfast-man's grin." His resistance to both groups shapes his development from good loyalist to Protestant nationalist.

Like other nineteenth-century Irishmen, yet unlike the leaders of the Literary Revival, JBY sees the "pure Irish," the bulk of the southern population, in religious rather than ethnic terms; for him they are Catholics more than they are Celts. He compares them, almost always favorably, to the Protestants of Belfast, London, and, later, New York. Modern Protestants are preoccupied with "*how to make a living*," Irish Catholics with "how to live." While they are concerned with money, power, and moral uplift, the authentic Irishman, he told audiences in New York and Philadelphia, throws his energy "into contemplation and desire" and seeks "visions of beauty and peace and hope and consolation." In Ireland there is rich enjoyment, an "abundance and variety of human nature" that is "still a bird uncaged." The native Irish are characterized on the one hand by sympathy and strength of intuition, on the other by a capacity for loyalty and service.

It is an affectionate and generous portrait, and in some ways a patronizing and sentimental one. If you use "the Irish" as a way to describe the limitations of Ulstermen, Englishmen, and Americans, you may be more kindly than critical. A member of the landlord class (though small and unsuccessful) who can both impoverish and love his Catholic neighbors, and who can recognize that he is doing both, is likely to make them figures in a rather unsatisfactory pastoral play. A man who spends the last fourteen years of his life away from home may be more nostalgic than analytic. *Early Memories* was written in New York, as was "The Soul of Dublin," his last essay, published thirteen days after his death in 1922. Both sentimentalize the Irish and so avoid really facing the historic responsibility of the landlords. When JBY writes of "the Island that used to be, when poverty, conversation, and idleness kept company with each other around the turf fire in the winter, or on the hillside in summer," he transforms the people into beings legendary and heroic, or Shakespearean and poetic, or both: "The soul of Ireland was partly pagan and that was good for lovers and for sensuous poetry; partly Catholic and Christian and that was good for the sorrowful and for lovers also; and partly patriotic and that was good for the courageous, whether young or old." He does recognize that there is also salt in the Irish character, and one of his most pleasant passages celebrates "a perfectly disinterested, an absolutely unselfish love of making mischief, mischief for its own dear sake." He understands too that salt can turn to gall, mischief to bitterness; he knows that Irish laughter can be "iconoclastic, harsh, and terrible." Nevertheless, while his perception of native Ireland is similar to that of his son Jack and their friend Synge, it usually lacks Synge's edge as well as O'Grady's epic enthusiasm.

The particular slant of his view of Belfast or Sligo, Dublin or London, most depends upon his class and its history. "Anglo-Irish" is a term of convenience, abuse, pride and confusion. It has been used to attack all Irish Protestants and to praise them or apologize for them, as an emblem of confiscation and oppression, and as one definition of modern Irish nationalism. For JBY—who understood Swift, had a strong historical sense, and whose Irish ancestry began with Englishmen and Huguenots naturalized under Cromwell—the burden and the greatness of the Anglo-Irish past was very vivid. He came of age at Sandymount with all its Georgian associations. His standard of rational nationalism was "those 20 years from 1780–1800, when Ireland had her own government and held her own course." He admired Augustan "courage and honesty . . . a frank and unbridled animalism, with cock fighting and bull-baiting and every kind of blasphemy." He did not discover ancient and heroic Ireland, but his Ireland did reach back to Goldsmith and Grattan, Barrington and Swift.

The Anglo-Irish identity meant a strong family and class sense, a feeling for a tradition to be upheld and a position to be maintained. JBY once justified the Big House landlords as "our aristocracy," but he did not claim to be one of them. Unlike his son, he never made much of the Ormond connection, was proud of the fact that the Yeatses "have always all of us been in the same situation in life for many generations," and wrote quite seriously that his ideal society was "a society of *poor* gentlemen." He is loyal but not uncritical. He recognizes the anomalous and uncomfortable position of the Anglo-Irishman—"England disowned them and they disowned Ireland"—the sense of being an outsider in so many places at once. Reaching maturity in the fifties and searching for a career in the sixties, he understood a certain paucity of alternatives at home and grasped the need to face England boldly and directly. He also felt that pervasive yearning of the Irish artist and intellectual to achieve some kind of unity out of the experience of so many Irelands.

The best way, perhaps the only way, to achieve or at

least approximate that unity is by a kind of autobiographical integrity, a faith in the authenticity of one's own experience and history. This means, for JBY as for WBY after him, insisting upon the centrality of Anglo-Ireland in Irish history. As Swift began by speaking for "the true English People of Ireland" but most effectively spoke to "the whole People," the Yeatses incorporate Protestant heroes into the Irish mythology. They define the spirit or soul of Ireland by invoking Burke and Isaac Butt as well as Cuchulainn and O'Connell; they assert the connections between Georgian Ireland and the most sustaining qualities of the modern nation. For JBY the basis for unity, and its best metaphor, is the family situation and "the drama of a full home life." He compared the Irishman's love of place with the Englishman's pride in Empire and the American's sense of vastness. Burke had said that the nation was the home writ large; JBY reverses the emphasis—home is a little nation—and so includes Anglo-Ireland in the total Irish experience. When he wrote or talked of "the Irish home," he also meant "my home," and an essay for *Harper's Weekly* in 1911 is an idealized conflation of his father's home in Tullyish and his own in London and Dublin when the children were growing up. "Back to the Home: An Irishman's Reflections on Domestic Problems and Ideals" celebrates family and place, "the old delicious autocracy with its smiling court of sympathetic and affectionate guests." The Irish family provides a small and stable unit immeasurably more fruitful than the stiff upper lips and minds of British public schools or the "delirious collectivism" he found in the United States. Unified by affection, habit, and tradition, it permits the growth of an individuality rather than the production of a "mere wheel or pulley in some immense machine . . . controlled by a cold-blooded arithmetician." It encourages pride, independence, and the desire and feeling for personal distinction. It fosters lively and endless conversation, and from conversation come curiosity, spontaneity, audacity, and hence "the valour of the free intellect." It is the custodian of "the conditions from which spring art and poetry." It is neither surprising nor, finally, limiting that JBY has been remembered as the father of genius.

2

London and Dublin

Meanwhile, there was a career to make and a growing family to support. William Butler Yeats was born in 1865, followed, over the next six years, by Susan Mary ("Lily"), Elizabeth Corbet ("Lolly"), Robert, and Jack. JBY was called to the bar in 1866; but life in Dublin had turned a little sour since Robert Corbet's suicide and the sale of Sandymount; the law had never really appealed to him, and the example of elderly barristers without briefs was wholly depressing; he was restless and unsettled. He had always drawn well and, in 1867, he abandoned Dublin for London and law for art, studying in Heatherley's Art School for two years and then at the Academy School with E. J. Poynter.

The Pollexfens, solid and stolid men of business and position, were anxious for their daughter and her expanding family and annoyed with their son-in-law. At least one sister was convinced that he was entering a life of waste and wantonness, and old William Pollexfen— "like Napoleon unamusable," JBY recalled—steadily disapproved. On his part, JBY came to feel that his "tragedy" was being "a born painter—imprisoned in an imperfect technique," that he should have studied longer, and would have achieved mastery had it not been for family pressures to get on with a profession. So it is a mark of his fundamental generosity that, while he resisted and resented the pressures and had a strong sense of personal and family dignity, he rarely speaks of the Pollexfen prodding and dismay with real rancor. Still, it was a trying period. Between 1867 and Susan Yeats's death in 1900, JBY spent 26 of the 33 years in London, and the frequent changes of address suggest a difficult and nomadic life.

JBY's first commissions did not materialize until 1872, the year after Jack's birth, and the rents from his property in Kildare had been substantially depleted. (They were to go altogether in 1880.) For the rest of his career he had to live the brave and uncomfortable role of the serious artist rather out-of-pocket. Proud of his independence, he still hopes for portraits of the eminent and wealthy that would be hung in drawing rooms and galleries to attract the further attention of the eminent and the wealthy. He cheerfully mocks the values of the market-place but worries about his daughters, asks for loans, and learns to accept gifts gracefully. Anxious for commissions, he paints friends (or any interesting face) for nothing, elaborately avoids assignments from people he does not like, and leaves sketches scattered all over London, Dublin, and New York. One of his best portraits of the nineties is of Nannie Farrar Smith, for which he is paid, or rather presented, a used bicycle. He feels, correctly, that his prospects as a black and white illustrator are being preempted by improved photography, "being so much cheaper and better liked by the stupid people."

In *Reveries over Childhood and Youth,* WBY recalls that in those early days his father had torn the tail of his coat "that he might not be tempted from his work by society . . . and I have heard my mother tell how she had once sewn it up, but before he came again he had pulled out all the stitches." It sounds pleasant and bohemian. But WBY's memories of his mother's anxiety over children and money—"I always see her sewing or knitting in spectacles and wearing some plain dress"—suggest that the rips and repairs were necessary and embarrassing rather than casual and comfortable. JBY's letters sometimes strike a note just this side of desperation:

Tomorrow I am to have a long sitting from Mrs. Clement Shorter, and feel not a little anxious, as it draws towards the close the difficulties increase. In Shorter I have excited an expectancy and in Mrs. Shorter a possible impatience—in myself much confidence with fits sometimes of deadly sickening fear, the more so as I know how much depends on this particular effort. The situation is hemmed round with dangers. A few days ago Shorter happened to say his wife would not sit again for a week. I did not sleep that night till four in the morning. I was perfectly calm, perfectly cheerful but wide awake. One cannot take things at sixty as we do at thirty.

There were other sorts of frustration and disappointment. Elizabeth Yeats wrote laconically in her diary for September 8, 1888: "Wrote Papa's story at his dictation. A fine scene, I think. It is drawing to a close." JBY was exhibiting his paintings at the time, not selling many or receiving commissions, and so stretching his talents to meet his needs. Years later Jack Yeats told Van Wyck Brooks of the same or a similar episode: "As you mention courage, how about this? Once my father's eyes gave out momentarily and he believed that he was going blind. But, saying nothing about this, he called for my sister Lily and began dictating a novel to her. If he was no longer to be able to see to paint, he would turn himself into a writer and the sooner the better." The "blindness" may have come from overwork; it was almost certainly connected with the strain of family difficulties, most especially the series of strokes that his wife was then suffering.

For such a gregarious and energetic spirit, he was, during the early London years, remarkably diffident. When Rossetti admired one of his paintings and sent three messages inviting him to call, he demurred and later regretted it. He went to art school with Samuel Butler, whose talent and prickly humanity he admired, and yet he held back and later wrote in *Early Memories,* "I sometimes think I have lost all my opportunities; the chance of knowing Butler well was one of these." Browning liked a design for "Pippa Passes" and came to visit, but he was out. A friend wanted to introduce him to Meredith but he declined. His compani ns were not the great and famous of late Victorian London but congenial and interesting near-failures, "a little like becalmed ships," his son recalled.

In such diffidence is self-reliance and self-protection; like Keats, JBY is unwilling to risk the lessened identity that usually accompanies discipleship. In his frustration and disappointment there is still great hopefulness; that "one good portrait" which would make his career is a continuing note of his early letters, as "my father doing well or about to do well" is of his son's. In his improvidence there is a certain wry strength.

Like his sons, he is constantly beginning, always on the verge of new discoveries and accomplishments. When he was eighty-one years old and WBY assumed liability for his support in New York, JBY wrote: "At last I shall be able to put aside money-making and acquire skill, as a palmist advised me to do years ago." The following year, four months before his death, he daily came bounding upstairs, he reported, all eagerness to be at work on his self-portrait; it was to outshine all paintings in New York, and he was again delaying passage home until its completion.

JBY's buoyancy depends partly on the family, its affection and coherence. Chesterton's recollection is avuncular and patronizing—"the intensity and individualism of genius itself could never wash out of the world's memories the general impression of Willie and Lily and Lolly and Jack; names cast backwards and forwards in a unique sort of comedy of Irish wit, gossip, satire, family quarrels and family pride"—but the gaiety, shrewdness, and pride are all there, confirmed by other visitors, family memories and letters, and by JBY's celebration of the Irish home. As the natives of Sligo had dug in and consolidated, so the Yeats family, abroad in alien London or not quite at home in suburban Dublin, stayed close, supportive and united. Though they were in their way wild geese, intellectually restless and eager for experience, they all envied rooted men (Pollexfens, Middletons, Synge), and home—for all the changes of address, parades of visitors, and extended absences—was their community.

There were domestic trials and separations, but there was also immense vitality and, eventually, triumph.

After Robert's death from the croup in 1873, JBY stayed on in Sligo and undertook the education of his eldest son that was to continue for twelve years and become such a central theme of *Reveries over Childhood and Youth*. WBY was a wandering and wayward student, and his father an unorthodox and impatient but persistent and resourceful teacher. He read out poetry on a spit of land that juts into the sea between Sligo and Rosses Point and later over breakfast in his York Street studio. They went to *Hamlet* together and JBY rehearsed Balzac's plots; but they soon progressed from stories to style, JBY characteristically endorsing the passionate and the concrete, and "always looking for the lineaments of some desirable, familiar life." He returned the family to Dublin in 1880 partly because living was cheaper there, but also—it seems likely—because William was fifteen and it would be better to come of age and try to begin a literary career at home. He wrote to Dowden in 1884, "so far I have his confidence. That he is a poet I have long believed, where he may reach is another matter," and together they arranged a few subscriptions so that *Mosada*, a Moorish tale in verse, could be published in 1886. Throughout the period he encouraged each of his son's efforts to become an imaginative writer and tried to help him resist the temptations, including money, of literary journalism.

The girls grew up and were patient, tactful, and yearning, feeling a little out of it away from Ireland and among all those voluble males, trying to keep life on a relatively even keel, to help foster an atmosphere that would permit contention and growth without envy or rancor. They were also exploring and defining their own possibilities; Susan Mary studied embroidery with May Morris, whose assistant she became, and experimented with spiritualism; Elizabeth taught art and wrote stories, which she submitted to journals like the *Vegetarian*. JBY encouraged his daughters and insisted upon their right to whatever careers they could make, and these activities led to the establishment of the Dun Emer (later Cuala) Industries in 1901, surely one of the most admirable cottage industries of modern Ireland. Jack lived in Sligo most of his youth, came to London in the eighties, began to prosper as a black and white artist, married a fellow student in 1894, and settled in Devonshire. Like his friend John Synge, he was a traveler and a listener, less restless than his father and brother, deeply rooted in Sligo and then Devon, and able to accept and celebrate life as it came.

In 1888 the family returned to Bedford Park, an artist's colony of red brick houses built by Norman Shaw, full of talk, activity, and children. The comfortable house at 3 Blenheim Road, with a balcony overlooking a garden shaded by a large chestnut tree, was the last house in which the Yeatses were consistently together. It remained vivid in their memories and in the impressions of many visitors: the family sitting for JBY, reading aloud and debating ("Papa and Willie had a hot argument on metaphysics"); going off to French lessons and exposure to English socialism at William Morris's establishment at Hammersmith; Jack coming and going, bringing treats, shouting Sligo nonsense rhymes, and delighting everyone; WB off to see Morris or Madame Blavatsky or an editor, attending meetings, founding societies, being enraptured by

Maud Gonne, the more so because she argued politics with JBY. The tone is slightly bohemian, adventuresome but still genteel, vigorous, often homesick, and very affectionate. It is held together by JBY's one undisputed genius—for talk: his "soft flexible voice" controlling the tempo and direction of endless conversation, rapid and cheerful, natural and rhythmic, often witty and mocking and contentious, but almost always tolerant and never mean. He still was not established as a painter, but his career as the best talker in town reached its first full fruition at Bedford Park.

His auditors were not always Yeatses, and one of the major compensations for life in London was a circle of lively companions. They too mitigated the frustrations of a shaky career and alien residence. During the 1870s JBY was one of a group that called itself "The Brotherhood," pre-Raphaelite in training and sympathy, believing in a union of the arts, and following Blake and Rossetti. The other members were John Nettleship, who also had abandoned commerce for art and went to Heatherley's and the Slade, a water-colorist who became an impressionist known for large paintings of lions; George Wilson, another water-colorist; and Edwin J. Ellis, erratic poet, painter, and eventual collaborator with WBY on the edition and interpretation of Blake. Other friends of the period were Frank H. Potter, a small man with a stutter who died of neglect and starvation and whose one well-known painting, "Dormouse," now hangs in the Tate with a catalogue note by JBY; and John Todhunter, the doctor turned minor poet, patron of JBY and his friends.

In the nineties JBY was a member of The Calumet

Club, a conversation group founded by Moncure Conway, which met every other Sunday evening and talked on into the early morning. Oliver Elton—the scholar, critic, and translator—was a member, as was Henry Paget, a painter and a boxer, reputed to be the strongest man in Bedford Park. Todhunter, Ellis, and Nettleship were still close, and other visitors included G. K. Chesterton, John O'Leary, R. A. M. Stevenson, and Florence Farr. JBY's greatest friendship was with York Powell, who became as important to him as Isaac Butt had been, and in similar ways. He was a model, a representative man defining significant virtues, as well as a close friend: "He had the same power of evoking affection, and he threw himself altogether into friendship as Butt threw himself into politics." Powell was the Regius Professor of Modern History at Oxford and a force in the development of Scandinavian and Medieval studies, but it was his unprofessorlike personality (*pace* Dowden) that JBY admired—his physical vigor, love of the sea and its folk and tales, his wide and odd knowledge. Even severe disagreements could not divide them; Powell was a Tory and an Empire man, JBY an acute critic of British imperialism, and the Boer war was grimly unfolding; but, after an intense argument, they agreed not to talk about it rather than risk separation. Powell's death in 1904 was a terrible wrench—"I feel now as if I had no friend left, he has made such a gap in my life"— and JBY never returned to London.

WBY rather resented his father's circle. Though none were abject, some were failures, none were conventional successes, and all were past great ambition. They talked for talk's sake, without special commitments or hostilities and without a sense of personal or public crisis. It annoyed the eager young man with such vast hopes and vulnerable ego. Their irresoluteness was in fact part of what attracted JBY to them, for it appealed to his social instincts and met a personal need. They approximated that society of poor gentlemen more interested in life than in achievement that he admired and almost succeeded in creating for himself.

They also helped him to revise—to sharpen and chasten—his view of England. He had come to London in 1867 imperfectly but genuinely educated, with all his Anglo-Irish biases, the acute and self-conscious outsider, an amateur anthropologist observing and typing the English race. He was, and remained, astute about their faults and quick to judge. He mocks the stolid English devotion to mediocrity and power, the lack of imagination, and the insularity. English self-assurance is "the happiness of a perpetual self-compla-cency. . . . such a self-complacency as only the killing off and the destruction of all the sympathies make possible; a high tide of personal and class conceit against which nothing can prevail." He argues that the "two great English facts" are "egoism and the legality by which each egoism protects itself against the encroachments of its neighbor egoism." Feeling the Irish experience, he is especially severe about British imperialism, a system, he writes, of selective and self-deceptive cruelty, "without pity and without chivalry," which is sustained by a "decorous hypocrisy" and "temporizing prudence" that manage to keep the victims out of sight.

JBY was also an enthusiastic reader of Mill and an honest man, and he acknowledges some characteristic

English virtues: a sense of personal liberty—"in his blood and in his bones"; a self-sufficiency that is not necessarily selfish; a skepticism and moral empiricism that distrusts Theories and Philanthropies but cultivates the "tenderness of humour" required to touch "healingly, all the sores of humanity". He found real companions and fruitful associations in England and had to mute the contradictions between his Irish patriotism and prejudice, on the one hand, and his friendships and the fundamental decency of his perceptions on the other. (During the Great War he became emphatically pro-British, partly from natural sympathy and partly from distrust of Germany and affection for France, and insisted that "the Irish must help *their English brothers*.") So he makes a working distinction between "the typical Englishman" and "the English gentleman"—"a rare species and now almost extinct . . . the most charming of companions and the truest of friends." In theory, "a gentleman is such simply because he has not got the doctrine of getting on and the habit of it. . . . The contest is not against material things, but between those who want to get on and those who don't want to get on, having other important things to attend to." As a matter of individual judgment, JBY usually reserves the approbation for the artist or scholar, or for the man who has sufficient leisure and intelligence to cultivate a lively and convivial interest in the arts. Like Veblen, he admires and wants to protect idle curiosity. He is not rigid or merely snobbish about it, and he is not fooled into thinking "the creed of being a gentleman" sufficient. He defended himself during a Royal Hibernian Academy debate, and doubtless would have defended others, on the grounds that "sometimes one is not a gentleman because one is something more important than a gentleman."

He is also fond of some conventional English types— "the aitchless majority," unlettered but "saturated with their own past and ancient history", the poor gentry and the country parsons. He likes the England of Fielding—robust, eccentric, and rural—and dislikes the urban and commercial world of Galsworthy. Just as he has searched in poetry for the definition of "some desireable familiar life," he finds in society the qualities already suggested by literature. His most important poets—Shakespeare, Shelley, Keats, Goethe—speak to him more or less directly, and he is inclined to collapse the usual distinctions between psychology, sociology, and aesthetics. (In this instinct, and in his essential view of England, he is surprisingly like George Orwell.) His "England"—complex object of affection and mockery, respect and loathing—is a creature of the imagination as well as of observation and historical sense.

In 1900 Susan Yeats died, and the following summer JBY moved back to Dublin with his daughters. It was to be the last family removal from London and the final return to a city that now looked rather promising. The Celtic Revival was well underway; there seemed a real chance that Irish nationalism could lead to reconciliation and unity rather than animosity; many people felt that the old city was going to become the locus of grace and culture that she had been late in the eighteenth century. Hugh Lane, an astute judge of painting, brought into the Irish movement by Lady

Gregory, was impressed by an exhibition and invited JBY to do a series of portraits of Ireland's political and intellectual leaders. During the next seven years his career as a painter reached its qualified fulfillment.

He had come a long way since Heatherley's School, starting with a pre-Raphaelite and romantic bias, but soon becoming more realistic and representational— the fine, large chalk portrait of Butt, done around 1875, marks the change. In 1882 he did a series of drawings of the Phoenix Park murder trials and, two years later, two of his best paintings, "The Bird Market" and an interpretive portrait of a consumptive beggar girl who came with other children to his studio at Stephen's Green. He exhibited at both the Royal Academy in London and the Royal Hibernian Academy (of which he became an associate in 1887 and a member in 1892) and did his first series of portraits of Dublin notables: Dowden, Sir Andrew Hart (Vice-Provost of Trinity), Lord Justice Fitzgibbon, Judges Monroe and Madden. According to Katharine Tynan—whose portrait he also did—JBY could have become a kind of court painter to the Dublin establishment. But he resisted—probably because of the political implications, certainly because of his own prickly independence, and perhaps because the prospect of oppressively steady employment unsettled him more than the financial worries. He charged ridiculously small fees and never wholeheartedly courted success. It is a minor emblem of his career, as Hone reports, that his portrait of Madden (the scholar, not the judge) together with his first wife was delivered on the very day that Madden married his second wife.

During the late eighties and nineties, JBY was primarily a black and white illustrator. (He wrote to his son that "from 1890 to 1897 I never touched a paint brush.") He did the drawings to accompany *In Memoriam* for the *Leisure Hour,* others for *Good Words,* and a series of forty-eight illustrations for Dent's sixteen-volume edition of Defoe. These wash-drawings, which are skillfully done and genuinely illuminate both character and story, pictured Crusoe, Singleton, and the rest for a whole generation of readers. (The presentation of Moll Flanders, save for one exuberant dance, suggests that JBY restrained himself for his late-Victorian audience. Dent said that all the figures except Friday look like Lily Yeats, who was her father's sitter, but he exaggerates.) In 1893 he provided the frontispiece for *The Celtic Twilight* and in 1897 the frontispiece and drawings for five of the stories of *The Secret Rose.* They are not distinguished. In spite of his beginnings and his son's interests, JBY is not a literary painter. These drawings and "King Goll," also illustrating one of WBY's poems, are his only contributions to the Celtic Twilight. His gift is mimetic and interpretative, not poetic, his interest in representation not story. He soon wearied of literary subjects and often left them unfinished, to the annoyance of his son. He is a natural portrait painter, competent illustrator, and a master of the sketch; so his return to portraits in 1898—"believing my salvation to lie that way"—is a recognition of talent and scope as well as resignation to the facility and popularity of photography. He was soon doing lots of them in Dublin, now competing with William Orpen rather than the photographers. He wrote to WBY in 1904, "I have been painting Miss

Lane in competition with Orpen, his style is learned—
like an old master, mine of course is modern and
impressionist; however I am satisfied that mine is the
better portrait." The "however" is properly pleased:
Orpen is twenty-five years old, JBY sixty-five. Lane's
commission led to his most permanent work (in both
senses of the phrase), until he bogged down around
1907. He did a few political figures such as Timothy
Harrington, Lord Mayor of Dublin, but mostly—and
most successfully—theater people and writers: Lady
Gregory, Anne Horniman, W. G. Fay, Horace
Plunkett, AE, WBY again, Padriac Colum, Standish
O'Grady, George Moore, and John Synge. A few of
these remain in private hands, but most are in the hall
of the Abbey Theatre, the Irish National Portrait
Gallery, and the Dublin Municipal Gallery.

In spite of JBY's frequent despondency about his
work, he seems always to have been ebullient when
painting. Dowden's description, allowing for the
teacherly resistance to wayward conversation, sounds
right:

> It is interesting enough to see Mr. Yeats at work—he
> gets so thoroughly into the "fluid and attaching" state,
> every glance at one's face seems to give him a shock, and
> through a series of such shocks he progresses. He finishes
> nothing, but gets his whole picture just into an embryo
> existence, out of which it gradually emerges by a series
> of incalculable developments; and all the while he is
> indulging in endless gossip of the peculiar *Yeatsian* kind, i.e.
> telling trivial facts and reducing them under laws of
> character founded on ethical classifications on down to
> Aristotle or any other student of character—classifications
> which are perpetually growing and dissolving!

He talked while he painted not only because he loved it and was good at it, but because he knew that conversation was part of his method, that "the genius of portrait painting is largely a genius for friendship." While he is anxious about his own imperfect technique, and admires craftsmanship and mastery, he always attacks mere technique, where facility submerges expression. The artist "with the full mind," he says, will attend wholly to his subject and simply, humbly hope that his technique will be "equal to his thought." He is more interested in color and representation than form, and cheerfully mocks the decorative, the excesses of Academy Painters, studio-bred. He is uncertain about modernism (especially cubism) because of its formalism and its fashionability, and he is equally severe with "moral uplift" and "art for art's sake."

The usual view of JBY—fostered by WBY's *Autobiographies* and hence by studies of the poet—is that he liked to talk more than he liked to paint, and that he was better at it. Accounts of his career are casual and secondary, agree with his own judgment about imperfect technique, and conclude that he was always a painter of promise rather than accomplishment, that "he stands, rather more evidently than most, for so much more than he delivered." His over-painting and inability to finish has become almost mythic through WBY's account of the pond at Burnham Beeches: "He began it in spring and painted all through the year, the picture changing with the seasons, and gave it up unfinished when he had painted the snow upon the heath-covered banks." The impression is supported by Katharine Tynan's recollections, by Dowden's remark to Todhunter than "the Eurydice [presumably a painting] belongs of right to him who can

bring her up from the hell of Yeats's studio," and by
John Sloan's impatience—normally affectionate but
sometimes testy—with his tinkering. JBY often painted
in Sloan's studio, and one day when the Sloans were
moving to another apartment, he painted on—and on—
until the workmen removed his easel and mirror from
the now-empty room. When he reported a fortune-
teller's prediction of steady employment, Sloan replied
that she must have been thinking about the self-portrait
that he began in 1911, and which was not quite finished
when he died eleven years later. "It fills my life," he
wrote in 1921; "I have never an idle moment or idle
thought. It is a long revel, just as satisfying to me as
Gibbon's 'Decline and Fall of the Roman Empire,'
and I think I have been at it almost as many years.
This morning I scraped away all the paint, but now
it looks very promising."

While it is certainly true that JBY talked and fussed
and delayed, and probably true that his promise as a
painter exceeded his achievement, both truths have been
overworked. His self-deprecations and the anecdotes
that cluster around him have obscured the fact that he
matters as a painter, that he was a serious and significant
artist. He was admired and encouraged by a wide range
of very good judges: academic critics like Thomas Bodkin,
Director of the National Gallery of Ireland and Professor
of Fine Arts and Director of the Barber Institute;
successful painters like Sarah Purser, Augustus John,
and John Sloan; major collectors like Hugh Lane and
John Quinn. Sloan said that JBY and Robert Henri
were "the two great influences in my life." Lane's
interest in Irish art and culture was partly sparked by

his exhibit of 1901. Quinn purchased and publicized his work and depended on his judgment. Surely one of the measures of success should be the people a man tangibly affects and those whose respect he earns. It is no small accomplishment to have been important to America's foremost painter and to two of the most adventuresome and discriminating collectors of the twentieth century. They liked him because of his natural charm and human warmth, but they also respected his work. "He is a fine unspoiled artist gentleman. His vest is slightly spotted; he is real," wrote Sloan after meeting him; and "artist" carries almost as much weight as "real" and more than "gentleman."

His limitations are clear, have largely to do with technique and will power, and he acknowledged them. His best sketches are marvelous in their verisimilitude and vitality, their sense of movement and character. His portraits are informed by a sure instinct, a respect for and understanding of his sitter, and by broad sympathy and human interest. He is an unusually *thoughtful* portrait painter—both considerate and reflective. Bodkin writes well about his special and difficult accomplishment, "an air of mingled intimacy and dignity that no other portrait painter of modern times surpasses," except, perhaps, Gustave Ricard. His paintings of young WBY, O'Leary and Butt, Synge and George Russell are an authentic part of modern Irish culture.

3

New York

Early in 1909, Lady Gregory wrote from Coole Park to John Quinn in New York, and commiserated about the burden of JBY: "It is wonderful how hopeful, how cheerful, how impossible he is. I admire him immensely at a distance, and I think him the most trying visitor possible in a house. Space and time mean nothing to him, he goes his own way, spoiling portraits as hopefully as he begins them, and always on the verge of a great future! I should lock up his paints and only allow him a pencil, and get occasional rapid sketches from him."

That letter, with its affection rather overcome by its condescension, and its refusal to take his work seriously, says much about JBY's situation in Dublin after the turn of the century, and about the tone the city adopted toward him. It was a situation and a tone that he needed to escape. Most of his portraits had been exhibited but he was neither successful nor self-assured. He might have become the establishment painter or another recorder of the Literary Revival, but he was too proud and his instincts too sound for either role. His wife and some of his old friends were dead. His sons were independent and well on their way to major success; and WBY could be cruel. ("I wish Willie . . . did not sometimes treat me as if I was a black beetle," he complained in 1904.) Even when there were good intentions all around, it was wearing to be known as the father of his sons. Much later he wrote to WBY and said "it was as bad to be a poet's father as the intimate friend of George Moore."

So, when Lily Yeats, the child with whom he had perhaps the warmest and certainly the most comfortable relations, went to New York to show her embroidery in 1908, JBY went too. Hugh Lane, Andrew Jameson, and other Dublin friends had assembled a fund so that he could travel to Italy and experience the great collections ("think of it," Sarah Purser said, "J.B. has never seen the Florentine galleries or the Vatican"); but he sailed for America instead. Lily returned to Ireland alone, and JBY, in spite of loneliness and yearning and many false starts, remained in New York until his death in 1922.

He was by no means free of money worries and still felt caught in a kind of bondage to the idea of a career. His first letters home from New York speak of "success—real success" with his sketches and of hopes for commissions to paint portraits. He is extending himself, writing essays and making speeches, convinced "that if I could venture a little, hire a studio for instance, I should soon be in full employment." But soon there are some grim notes: "All my life I have chased the chimera of success, and sometimes the chimera of art." One odd mischance or another means lost commissions and missed connections: "Living here thinking about articles which won't come and waiting for promised letters from promising patrons which don't come either is a little dreary." He has to accept gifts gracefully, usually from WBY or John Quinn, who sometimes simply send him money and sometimes invent transparent stratagems to assist him. Quinn purchased many of the poet's manuscripts, beginning in 1914, with the understanding that some of the proceeds would support JBY. He presented him with tickets home, which JBY redeemed and which thus became an indirect and sporadic subsidy. Age, frustration, and improvidence combine to produce a note of pathos that even extraordinary good humor cannot altogether distance: "If I were forty years younger I could be a great success. An old artist seeking work is like a ticket-of-leave man looking for a situation—either of them might run away with the spoons!"

His sons are on their own and doing well, but he does worry about the girls, especially about Lily who, he says ruefully, "would be buying embroideries instead of making them" if his commissions could be realized. He dreams a great deal, which he attributes to a diet of fruit, claret, bread, and no meat, but he knows that food is only a proximate cause, and the dreams are not usually tranquil. Lily has told him that dreams of living fish signify money, and he soon dreams of fishing at Coole and catching one so large that it nearly pulls him in. He writes WBY in the spring of 1915 that Quinn has rescued him again, at least for the moment, "so I am now financially quite comfortable—which is a great deal—even if my conscience is not at all comfortable. I dreamed last night that I had a visit from your grandfather who asked me how long I expected him to support me." Like other men he generalizes and makes philosophic the dimension and the feel of his own situation: "The true artist when he paints a sunrise or sunset knows that he has failed—of one thing only certain, that the copy resembles hardly at all the original. . . . This sense of failure is the melancholy of artists. It is their appointed agony." Underneath the generalizations there is a personal reality not so much harsh as constricting and embarrassing. His last letter to John Quinn, written six days before he died, is full of good spirits about his self-portrait, his appearance before the MacDowell Club, "a very clever and pretty young lady" he is sketching, and his wanderings about New York in the cold winter. But it begins: "My dear Quinn—Many thanks for the $30. I have been badly wanting underwear and socks."

His loneliness is compounded by a deep homesickness. Within a year he is writing to friends and family, answering their entreaties to return, that he would like to come home, to escape the "fever" of New York, if only it could be "peace with honor." The "gambling excitement" of America's possibilities holds him, and the strongly recollected dread of "impending insolvency" in Dublin forestalls him. But increasingly he writes, especially to his old friend Ruth Hart (Mrs. Andrew Jameson), of the "powerful home-returning instinct" that possesses him. He celebrates Ireland to his friends and urges them to visit, seizes upon travelers from home, pleads for letters, and is sorely disappointed when they do not arrive. He is immensely excited about WBY's visits in 1911, 1914, and 1920 and, always, dreams about home. Though he never loses faith in the New World, or fascination with its ways, thoughts of Ireland can make him sour. "A sort of European old-maidishness gets between me and them," he writes about young Americans, and as the years go by and the generational landmarks accumulate—death of friends, marriage of their children, birth of their grandchildren—the yearning becomes acute and sustained. Living in New York is extraordinary, but he wants to die at home. It would be glorious to return "to tell my traveller's tales"—yet he suspects that no one would listen.

Dublin certainly tried to get JBY to return, countless times and in many tones. Lily implored, WBY proposed, and Quinn purchased tickets. AE soon found the city "desolate" without him and suggested in 1908 that they cable "Family all dying. Come to receive last messages." Susan Mitchell later complained that "conversation has become a lost art in Dublin since he left it; people only gabble now," and she threatened to come to America and bring him back by the hair of his head. But feelings and events intervened: first his anxiety about what life in Dublin would really be like, then the war, then inertia combined with his sense of promises to keep and achievements to record in New York. So the "old man who ran away from home and made good" never did return.

New York had distanced that bondage to a career. It was no more home than London had been, but not much less, and it was revitalizing, a superior form of exile. As Jack Yeats noticed, his circles were limited in Dublin, but in New York there were circles within circles to explore, and JBY plunged into them. One night he went to Coney Island with Quinn, Sloan, and Ezra Pound where, after dinner and talk, they all shot the chutes and rode in the tubs. He took Sloan on an all-day hike to cure a lame back, beginning on Riverside Drive, taking the street-car to Van Cortland Park, on to

Yonkers, on the ferry across the Hudson, and climbing and walking out into the Hackensack Valley. He went to see Buffalo Bill in Madison Square Garden, baseball in Harlem, and to the old Astor Library with Sloan, who became more interested in the scrubwomen than the books, and so began one of his most memorable paintings. When he was knocked down by a streetcar in 1918, Quinn wrote the family that "your father was, as usual, strolling through the traffic of New York like an Emperor in his garden." He was unfailingly alive. When Sloan complained that shortened skirts were a failure because there were so many ugly ankles, he replied, "I am surprised to hear you say that, Sloan. I think they're all beautiful, and I'm glad I've lived to see them."

A year and a half after his arrival he wrote an article that celebrates New York and his own special response: "It is the old man's paradise—the old man who is always an underdog. Here not only does he catch, by an infection he cannot resist, some of the vivacity of youth, but he comes in time to fancy himself almost young and a sharer in his neighbor's hopes." He writes with particular affection about the American climate (except for the mosquitoes, and he soon added other reservations), faces (the painter's eye at work), vitality, humor, and courage. Living in the intellectual and commercial center of an English-speaking nation not British recalled his undergraduate response to the humane and optimistic liberalism of Mill: "What he thought in grave abstract speech I find here every where in the rich fruitage—glowing to the eye, acid sweet to the taste, and by its fragrance attracting round it many humming bees." Such valiant, happy notes persist throughout his life in New York and qualify and soften the lonely and forlorn moments. He wanted very much to be optimistic and often, convincingly, was:

> I am in my 75th year and feel that life is just beginning; 45 years ago a lady cunning about the future told me that I would not win success till I was very old and that then it would be *universal* success; what she meant by universal success, I could not guess, but now I know—since I sometimes sketch in pencil, sometimes paint, sometimes lecture, and sometimes write articles, and sometimes am well paid and sometimes am badly paid—every kind of experience.

In nineteenth-century London he had always felt the Anglo-Irish outsider and liked to play the role of detached and occasionally acid observer. In New York he is still a visitor, and most observant, but the tone has changed. He is more relaxed, convivial, and generous, an amateur physiognomist and anthropologist studying the faces and charting the curious habits of the natives, a Hibernian Tocqueville still exploring the New World. He wrote five articles for *Harper's Weekly* on American life, and his letters are filled with sharp and sympathetic observations. He likes its helpfulness and tact and friendliness—"not a croaker in all New York, except here and there an unhappy Englishman who only gets laughed at for his pains, unless he turns very crusty, when he is dropped out of notice and out of memory." He joyfully discovers other un-British characteristics, especially the "weak sense of law and of property" and the lack of class consciousness. He admires "the open ingenuous and *wide* mind of the American which nothing startles and nothing frightens," its enthusiasm, energy, and optimism: "Hope, the great divinity, is domiciled in America, as the Pope lives in Rome."

Like Tocqueville, he is unsettled by American restlessness and finds not a society, but a conglomeration of "delirious activity," a "noisy picnic" of opinion, progress, and oratory that achieves pleasure instead of happiness and association rather than friendship, and that finds itself, willy-nilly, living on the surface. During the Great War he complains that "Emerson said that every man is a man of genius if he only knew it, and this has had a most deleterious effect on American civilisation—it is protestantism gone mad." New York has its own forms of the Puritanism and commercialism he had rejected in Belfast and London, an exaggerated idea of Service and Moral Improvement: "Being uplifted is the American recreation—with this kind of exercise they make their blood quite thin and colourless."

His reservations all hinge on his sense that American life is somehow and unintentionally inimical to poetry and art. Its "worship of cleverness" and capitulation to the tyranny of the practical breeds men and women who lack intellectual intensity and curiosity because they do not have, or will not take, the leisure sufficient to cultivate them. They are so "mad for justice" that they do not value liberty, and JBY emphasizes that he is talking about intellectual and artistic liberty: "What America needs to rescue it from its unrest and delirious collectivism is *poets and solitaries*, men who turn aside and live to themselves and enjoy the luxury of their own feelings and thoughts." That is a sustained note of his commentary on America, and so is the more carefully balanced judgment he sent to Harriet Jameson (complete with sketches) soon after his arrival: "Remember I am as much in love with the country as ever. They don't understand art and have no manners, but there runs through all ranks a goodness and kindness, and their humour is all based on this kindness. It is as if the stern countenances of the Pilgrim Fathers had [metamorphosed] into a grim mother, full of pity . . . pity but yet no indulgence."

JBY was intrigued by the American woman. He could joke that she is a "temple—carved out of blanc-mange"; but he could also celebrate: "A princess here is like a princess out of the wood—she has the dew of the morning on her hair and on her brow, a Diana rather than an Aphrodite—and she carries a spear." Two of the *Harper's Weekly* essays are delighted looks at the spear and the way she carries it. He genuinely admires the suffragette and contrasts her with her English counterpart, like Mrs. Humphrey Ward, whose female solidarity, he argues, is badly undercut by class snobbery. He praises her determination to be "un-ladylike" when necessary, and he takes an old man's puckish pleasure in "the woman interested in herself: surely it is a new thought. . . . It is all wonderful and beautiful, and the men are full of anxiety."

About politics generally, JBY is occasional, inconsistent, and very human. A wayward rationalist who remembers the impact of Mill with care and affection, he is likely to be "liberal" in his causes and perspectives. He frequently calls himself a socialist and occasionally a radical, but he dislikes reformers, is impatient with "sour-faced socialists" and their programs, and his few

revolutionary sympathies are cultural rather than
political. He admires and responds to democracy's
hopefulness and buoyancy, but distrusts its bustle and
dogmatism and attacks the narrowness and intolerance
of the "collective mind" with its greedy and "dull spirit-
less employment." His attachments often seem aristocratic, praising personal pride and honor and protecting
leisure, art, and conversation. "The artist must always
be an aristocrat and disdain the street," he writes, but
adds almost immediately: "aristocracies are malign,
and the whole of Nietzsche is malign; so are college
dons and their retinue." Anxious lest WBY become
hermetic or simply snobbish, he writes in 1908:
"You have found yourself and found your public in
some of your plays, but not *quite triumphantly*. Democratic art is that sort which unites a whole audience . . .a
coterie of discontented artists may be something like
a tea-party of old maids discussing marriage and large
families—perhaps it is the narrow way that leadeth to
destruction." Unlike many men who endorse "aristocratic" values, he never betrays a contempt for human,
material wants, needs, or sufferings; and he never flirts
with authoritarianism: "The men whom Nietzsche's
theory fits," he again chastizes his son, "are only great
men of a sort, a sort of Yahoo great men. The struggle
is how to get rid of them, they belong to the clumsy and
brutal side of things."

JBY's only serious political involvement occurs
when he feels that politics are impinging upon art. He
supported Lady Gregory, Synge, and WBY during the
beginning and flowering of the Literary Revival. In
1918 John Quinn asked his help in preparing a brief to

present before the Ways and Means Committee of the House of Representatives, since Congress was again considering a stiff tax upon works of art. JBY wrote a long and persuasive letter attacking the commercial view of art and artists, defending their moral and intellectual seriousness, and asserting their essential contributions to the commonweal. Quinn won his major points. Otherwise, JBY is not vitally interested in politics, and his response to public issues is particular and empirical rather than programmatic. His politics are literary and whimsical, or pastoral. His utopia is not aristocratic, democratic, or socialist, but a shifting mediation among contending forces, a series of fluctuating and eclectic compromises, a set of shrewd yet wistful reactions to fashionable opinion.

JBY continued to paint in New York, but he was not a success, and painting (except for the self-portrait) occupies a less-and-less central place in his life. He wrote a good deal, more than he had in England or Ireland. Between 1909 and 1922, when he was in his seventies and early eighties, he wrote over a dozen essays, six of which were collected, along with one from 1907, in *Essays: Irish and American* (published in 1918). He published at least four reviews, two poems ("like Homer . . . only his are much longer"), and the recollections of his youth printed in 1923 as *Early Memories: Some Chapters of Autobiography.* He suppressed some additional chapters because he felt they would be as painful to read as they had been to write, and he composed at least two short stories and all or part of a play that were never published. WBY prodded and conspired for a longer autobiography, but JBY lost interest; he enjoyed talk-

ing about the past but preferred writing about the
present. Even that was difficult enough: "I have been
living mostly by writing," he wrote Mrs. Jameson
in 1913, "and compared to painting portraits I hate
writing," no casual statement for him. He worried
over an article: "It has given me a lot of trouble. Sometimes writing about a subject is like a sailor on a yard
single-handed furling a huge sail in a gale of wind—pa-
tience and strength and cunning, all necessary, while
the sail is trying to fling him into the sea, and will do
so if luck does not help as well." His career as a writer
is no more triumphant than his career as a painter, and
his *oeuvre* is neither substantial nor compelling. It is
nevertheless alert, honest and engaging, and his prose
was admired by some very discriminating judges—
Pound, Van Wyck Brooks, Lady Gregory, Susan
Mitchell—as well as by loyal members of the family.

He was an indefatigable correspondent and produced
several hundred letters to family and friends in Ireland
and America (representative though incomplete
selections were edited by Ezra Pound in 1917, Lennox
Robinson in 1920, and Joseph Hone in 1944). He gained
a minor reputation as a public speaker in eastern
United States and was known to a small but dedicated
circle as the best conversationalist in New York. He
was also a true friend, loyal companion, and fatherly
presence. He had left behind one son who was already
Ireland's foremost poet and another who was to become her foremost painter. So, around 1910, he became
father to Van Wyck Brooks, who was beginning his
career as man of letters and articulator of American
literary movements, and to John Sloan, America's

greatest painter. Both men record his real and paternal importance to them at decisive moments in their lives. JBY was their O'Leary. Their testimony is moving and impressive and their relationship to JBY is one of the most pleasing aspects of his admirable noncareer.

"It seemed to me later," Brooks recalled of his Harvard days, "that I had never been touched by anyone's intellect until in 1909 I met J. B. Yeats,—the old Irish artist in whom I found a master." They liked each other immediately and JBY began a portrait, a characteristic choice of sitter, for Brooks was neither rich nor famous, but he was alert, a good talker, and a better listener. Characteristically, too, it went badly: "He was convinced that his first portrait of me was a failure. He had come to my office in the rain in despair, so depressed that he could not sleep; and he sent me sketches of himself facing the canvas in hope, in exultation, in dejection and at last in triumph." The finished pastel sketch is rather vague and, as Sloan remarked about JBY's sketches generally, "a little sweet"; but it is appealing, and the eyes are full of life.

JBY was lonely in the new city and talk with a young and ambitious literary man was a distinct pleasure and met some needs. For Brooks the lively old man carried some of the glamor of the Irish Literary Revival and encouraged his hopes—"the fiddles are tuning all over America"—for a parallel movement in the United States. He admired JBY's openness, vigor, and sense of humanity, his "articulate talent, warmth of heart and wit." He delighted in the endless abundance of anecdote, perception, and fresh opinion: recollections of Isaac Butt, Samuel Butler, York Powell, and John O'Leary; stories about J. S. Mill's housemaid and about sin and redemption in Edinburgh; a summary of northern and Mediterranean attitudes toward women; views of American life and literature; a steady defense of artists and their prickly integrity. JBY taught his young friend, Brooks later recalled, two lessons: to "cherish the concrete," Blake's " 'minutely organized particulars,' words that I was to recall when the time came for me to write my history of the literary life in the United States"; and to distrust the trap of worldly success, to acknowledge if not quite embrace the "angel of impecuniosity" with her difficult freedom.

JBY's warmest friendship in New York was with John Sloan, whose diary for 1908–11 mentions him almost daily, full of affection and respect and appreciation for his "steady warm shower of reminiscences and ideas and kindliness and good humor." They eat, talk, paint, and read together, in Robert Henri's or Sloan's studio, at his Thanksgiving dinner, at JBY's hotel. JBY proudly reads out his son's poems and plays, or Lady Gregory's or Synge's, reports Irish news from letters, and describes the Irish scene from memory. He recounts dreams and omens and endorses fortune-telling, impressing but not convincing the skeptical Sloan, who nevertheless surprises and touches him with a copy of Cheiso's book on palmistry. They walk together all over the city and take tours to New Jersey, Westchester, and Philadelphia, the old and young artist leading each other on to new adventures and fresh perceptions of the vivid urban world.

Dolly Sloan loved JBY as fully as her husband did, and needed him more. Pretty and lively, orphaned daughter of Irish immigrants, estranged Catholic, she

was devoted to Sloan. But, deeply insecure, she felt
inferior to his frends; afflicted by melancholy and
drink, she was without children or regular work, often
painfully ill, always a patient, and occasionally driven
to suicide attempts. JBY loved Dolly and recognized her
qualities and her needs. He praised her loyalty, vitality,
and domesticity and tried to persuade her to see herself
as he did, saying that she had no pretense or ostentation,
but "the courage of the devil." Once she secretly demon-
strated both courage and attachment by going to WBY
when he was in town with the Abbey Players and appealing for more substantial support for his father. Her re-
ception at the hotel was brief and chilly, and her husband's
subsequent remarks about the poet are vague and
distant.

JBY did several pencil or pastel sketches of Sloan and
Dolly and often worked in Sloan's studio, a companionship that the younger man liked but found a
mixed blessing. The talk was disconcertingly good and
the painting disturbingly unconcentrated. JBY immediately recognized Sloan's genius and gave steady
advice and enthusiastic praise. He persuaded Quinn, well
before Sloan was fashionable, to buy a large group of
etchings and helped in the selection. He told Oliver
Elton in 1911 that "England and America have produced
only two serious painters; Hogarth and Sloan—(not including Blake, who was more poet than painter) and not
including landscape painters." He did two reviews of
Sloan's work in 1917, for *The Seven Arts* and *Harper's
Weekly,* and another for *The Freeman,* which appeared
a month before he died. Sloan demonstrates and defines
his idea of the major painter, the transforming and in-

terpreting personality that, following the dictates of both imagination and humanity, serves the instinct for order, peace, and beauty, and at the same time is devoted to the facts and their drama. He creates out of his own genius without denying its location in time and space. He is the "historian of New York" as well as America's only serious painter.

On his part, Sloan said that JBY was "the most acute and prophetic critic of my work" and, along with Henri, the major influence on his development. Henri, in the early stages, had insisted that the artist should study life; JBY, countering Henri and some of his own instincts as well, urges him to attend more fully to art, form and line. He chastizes Sloan for a certain carelessness, a damaging lack of concern with details, and insists that true art is greatly self-conscious, devoted to the "labor of premeditation" and the achievement of "realized form." He says that Renoir's figures are far ahead of Sloan's because Renoir had "looked longer at Rubens," and he prods Sloan to go to the museums and galleries as well as to the Astor Library and McSorley's tavern. He is anxious about the propagandist and activist in Sloan, admires his independence, and urges him to settle for "the quiet artist's courage, the courage to be himself."

This friendship was, Brooks recalls, "firm, complex and filial-paternal." At his funeral, Sloan and Brooks rode in the first coach and both men felt as if they had "lost a father." Those are Brooks's words; Sloan's letter to Elizabeth Yeats speaks for itself:

> That great man your father is no longer with us. . . . He has gone . . . and for me the world can never be the same. . . .

I assure you that my own father's death was not so great a loss to me. I was never as near to him as to John Butler Yeats. . . .

A few score men such as your father in the world at any one time would cure its sickness—but our civilization produces other flowers—unsavory blooms rank and poisonous— John Butler Yeats was one of the rare exceptions.

JBY's relationship to John Quinn, the man most responsible for bringing him to New York and most anxious about his health and material well-being there, was hardly filial-paternal. It was more like that between an old and penniless tutor and his wealthy, autocratic patron. If there is something appealingly early-modern about JBY's fathership of Brooks and Sloan, his life with John Quinn has a decidedly Victorian atmosphere. In 1902 John Quinn—successful lawyer, Tammany politician, aggressive collector—descended on Great Britain and appropriated the Yeatses and the Literary Movement. Jack took him around London, and the rest of the family, together with Lady Gregory, arranged his stay in Dublin. He began his long support of the Abbey Theater and Dun Emer Industries, purchased ten of Jack's paintings, and commissioned a series of portraits at £20 each from JBY. JBY's account of such frantic generosity strikes exactly the right note of real appreciation and tactful, ironic judgment that is to continue for twenty years of friendship. Quinn is "a newly arrived American" and "the nearest approach to an angel in my experience."

When Lily and her father landed in New York in 1908, Quinn met their boat, shepherded them through customs

and into a hotel, and set about providing clients, commissions, and connections (though JBY found his own
friends). Thereafter, until his death, JBY spent many
Sundays at Quinn's apartment, for lunch, the afternoon,
and a taxi ride home. They "did" New York—galleries,
museums, fine restaurants—and its environs—Fisher's
Island, the Jersey Palisades, Coney Island, and journeyed
together to Virginia and elsewhere on the east coast.
In 1917 JBY became seriously ill with influenza and
pneumonia and was cared for by Jeanne Robert Foster,
a woman of great beauty and intelligence, who had been
a school teacher, actress, and model, and was now a
writer and editor for the *Review of Reviews*. Quinn
helped as well, and so the illness brought him together
with the "good woman to rest his head" that JBY had
long prescribed. She was to become Quinn's companion
and the most important presence in his later life. JBY
was devoted to her—"It is so rare to find so much really
strong intellect with kindness and affection." She helped
him in dozens of ways, stayed with him throughout this
illness and the last one, and provided the plot in the
Adirondacks where he is buried.

JBY was more tolerant and affectionate than most
associates of the proud and combative Quinn, and more
honest and less afraid. He respected Quinn's judgment,
delighted in his brilliant career as patron and possessor;
Quinn excited the metaphorical in JBY's prose, and his
epithets are appealing and accurate: the "New World
Puritan," "a grand paymaster and a prompt one," a
"good storm tug," "the Schoolmaster," and, inevita-
bly, "the true deus ex Machina." Quinn was generous
and loyal, imperious and impatient, managerial and

scolding—New York's Lady Gregory. From the very beginning he tried inordinately hard to get JBY to go home, partly from a sense of obligation to the Yeats children, and partly from a busy man's resentment of yet another burden. Some of JBY's virtues—his relaxed, unsystematic, unhurried confidence—got on Quinn's nerves, which JBY recognized and occasionally tried to correct: "The fact is we both have nerves, only yours rouse your will into action, and they paralyse my will."

Furthermore, Quinn had a deep-seated aversion to the details of death, to corpses, hospitals, funeral arrangements, and bereaved relatives, and his increasing anxiety about JBY's "dying on my hands" seems almost pathological. That, of course, is just what happened, and Quinn, to his credit and with Mrs. Foster's help, did cope. He avoided the body but he did provide doctor and nurse, friends at his bedside, a dignified funeral, and orderly disposition of his few, lonely effects, like the crumpled letters from his children that he had carried about in his pockets until they were almost pulp. Quinn could not help grumbling—"Thank God, there is no Mrs. Yeats to come down to the office in black"—but he was kind and efficient and wrote the Yeatses a long and valuable memoir of their father's last days. He had been vigorous and happy to the end—entertaining at Petitpas and even dancing; reading a poem called "Autumn" to the MacDowell Club; visiting galleries with Quinn and Mrs. Foster. On Wednesday, February 1, Quinn, responding to a call from Mme. Jais, gathered Mrs. Foster and Dr. David Likely and found JBY in great pain. Dr. Likely diagnosed edema of the lungs and a weak heart, and thought that he could last only a few hours. Relieved

by injections of morphine and camphor, JBY slept well
and rested comfortably the following day, looking, Quinn
recalled, strong, erect, and brilliant. He died without
pain, just before seven A.M. on Friday, February 3,
1922.

JBY repaid Quinn's kindness in several ways. An entertaining companion, picturesque presence, and valued
correspondent, he was partly responsible for the education of the man of the world in the ways of art and the
imagination. He introduced Quinn, who knew little
about American art and was prejudiced against it, to
John Sloan. JBY put him in touch with the rest of "The
Eight" (a group of artists surrounding Robert Henri
who were to have an impact on the history of American
painting), and so with some of the serious work he had
not noticed going on around him in New York. As he
had done with Mrs. Foster, JBY brought Quinn to
people who helped him to grow. Meanwhile, he wrote
letters on all sorts of subjects, several hundred of them
between 1902 and 1922, which Quinn had typed before
attempting to read, and which he often let accumulate so
that he could answer four or five at once. They reveal
many of the same preoccupations, and language, as the
letters to WBY, and some observations and arguments—
little lectures—for Quinn's benefit. No doubt it was easier
to write to him in that vein than to talk with him. JBY
tactfully but forcefully explains that a patron is not a
bully, that he must accept the necessary, wayward independence of the artist: "After a while it will dawn on
you that it is only a Goth or a Philistine or *a man blinded*
by too much *friendship* . . . who would try to deprive
an artist of his right to paint his own way. It will soon be

revealed to you that the right is *inalienable* and that he *cannot be contracted* out of it." He offers intellectual generosity and disinterestedness to balance Quinn's lawyerly habit of attack ("You are a little too forensic."). He tries to account for some of the tricky relationships between the ego, creativity, and the aesthetic sense; to make distinctions among wit and humor and intellect; to elucidate his own beliefs about imitation and representation, style and form. He patiently suggests that Ireland, and especially her Church and her peasantry, are more complex than Irish-American enthusiasm allows. He continues his happy observations of America and her ways, enjoying his Tocquevillian role as much as the Arnoldian.

One of his most impressive tutorial efforts, because it involves growth as well as instruction, occurs in 1920. Many years earlier, in that essay on Irish life for *Harper's Weekly*, he had complained that "the Irish home, in which so much happens, awaits its novelist." In 1914 that novelist appeared, to everybody's surprise and almost everybody's chagrin, when *Dubliners* was published. JBY's first reaction was nervous and class-bound: "One always knew there were such persons and places in Dublin, but one never wanted to see them." He was puzzled and put off by *Portrait of the Artist as a Young Man*, but then, deeply moved by its sense of experience and entranced by its style, he committed whole passages to memory. Still, he had anxious moments: "Is Mr. Joyce a creative artist or the author of the squinting windows?" But now Joyce was under attack, struggling bravely and, it seemed, vainly to publish *Ulysses*, and Quinn was trying to help. On October 14,

JBY wrote a long essay-letter providing an argument. He begins by recognizing that the essential question is "whether the books of Joyce and such as he are to go free or not." His strong and affirmative answer is based on aesthetic, intellectual, and moral grounds. Joyce is a genius, a deep and subtle thinker, and an exceptional maker of prose: "Self-discipline of the sternest kind is evident in every sentence he writes. His influence is a bracing one." He does not write pornography, but difficult truth: "It is a Dantesque hardness and not a relaxed softness which inspires Joyce when he writes those so-called filthy passages. . . . The whole movement against Joyce and his terrible veracity, naked and unashamed, has its origin in the desire of people to live comfortably, and . . . superficially. It is impossible for any honest man who has given thought to the great issues of life to have any sympathy with this clamorous outcry." His writings may not make a man happier (do Shakespeare's?), but they will make him "wiser, and therefore stronger." JBY concludes autobiographically: "I know Dublin well. I know the pleasant falsehoods that are cherished by its good citizens, and I am not surprised to hear that they hate Joyce. . . . He should be helped and not hindered. No place needs him more than does Dublin." So also thought James Joyce, who would have been pleased with the letter. Its politics are salutary and its criticism just. It is an impressive spiritual act for an Anglo-Irish gentleman, aged eighty-one and away from home, to so appreciate and so defend. A year and a half later, on February 3, 1922, *Ulysses* was finally published in Paris on the day JBY died in New York.

John Quinn commissioned or purchased over a dozen of JBY's portraits and eventually returned most of them to the family or to one of the Irish cultural establishments. Predictably, the two most troublesome were the portrait of Quinn and the self-portrait. Soon after his arrival JBY began "his Quinn," promising that two or three sittings would suffice. After "eight solid Sundays," the busy lawyer issued his orders: JBY could have one more hour for the eyes, one for the hair, and so on, and he had to place the easel closer to his subject so that he could not pause, pace, and talk so much. The portrait was finally completed to neither man's satisfaction. "It has," a friend said, "a rather worried look."

In self-defense and apology, and recognizing that the old artist needed to linger, Quinn commissioned the self-portrait. JBY could take as long as he wanted and name his own price. Like everybody else, Quinn became distressed and impatient as the work dragged on. To the artist's comment, eleven years later, that it was still "in a very embryonic condition," Quinn replied that it was indeed a "venerable embryo . . . dangerously overdue." But JBY, stubbornly and beautifully, stuck to his task. The self-portrait nursed him out of what he liked to call, at eighty-two, "premature old age," and brought him up the long stairs to his rooms "with a bounding step." His letters to Quinn and WBY during his last four years make quite clear the kind of investment he felt: "In it I will live in my habit as I lived and it will hold its own among your masterpieces. It is an honest portrait." It embodies his professional pride, and he is right about how good it is; it gives him a reason to refuse to be hustled back home when he is not sure he is ready to go; it justifies his apparently aimless but actually quite purposeful sense of himself. It is, in real ways, his connection with life.

4

Wisdom

One of the happiest tangible consequences of JBY's residence in New York is John Sloan's "Yeats at Petitpas," painted during the summer of 1910 and now in the Corcoran Gallery, Washington, D.C. It shows Celestine Petitpas, dark and very pretty, bringing fruit to a table set with bottles of wine and glasses. At its head sits JBY, erect and alert, sketch-book in hand and one of Quinn's cigars in his mouth, surrounded by the Sloans, Brooks, the young poet Alan Seeger, and other friends and members of what was sometimes called (though not by him) "Mr. Yeats's circle." It included, at various times, the painters Robert Henri, George Bellows, William Glackens, and George Luks; visiting Irishmen and women like Padriac and Mollie Colum and Charles Johnston; and the Irish-American journalists Frederick James Gregg and Charles Fitzgerald. JBY sketched, recollected, reported, pronounced, gently debated, thoroughly enjoyed himself, and complained whenever anyone left early. Though he ate sparingly and drank only a little red wine or French vermouth, he liked to say that his idea of perfect bliss was the second drink of Jameson's stabilized forever. He chortled to Quinn that at a party to celebrate the New Year of 1913 he was kissed by all the girls—"the years bring their privileges." His life was bound up with his young friends and he shared their busy optimism, their sense that New York was "a huge fair," the center of an expansive and energetic artistic and intellectual life.

After staying at various hotels, he had moved into the small boarding house at 317 West 29th Street frequented by actors, writers, and tourists. There he remained until his death, the friend and concern of three sisters from Brittany. Marie Petitpas was Cook and Manager—"she is the brains"; Josephine was "the 'chucker-out' and keeps order and looks after the bills." The youngest, Celestine, was the beauty and the menial, waiting on table and cleaning the rooms. Of course, she was his favorite: "Her English is imperfect, but her manners are exquisite—she looks a Sylph among these fat German-American women—and her voice sounds so courteous and musical among these nasal voices." The hotel passed into other hands around 1920, those of Madame Jais, who was blunter and less lively than the sisters, but more efficient and in some ways more generous; she kept JBY's room warm during his last winters and helped him through illness. Celestine married and at last established her own home. JBY visited her regularly, shared her happiness, and eagerly worked on a life-sized portrait. He thought it "far and away the best portrait I have painted," and—typically—it was his gift to the sitter.

Like most ambitious and talented young men, Brooks and Sloan were skeptical about their elders and distrusted sages. Yet they found in JBY an old man they could admire and from whom they could learn, and a sage who

was sufficiently lively and skeptical—and vulnerable
enough to charges of failure—to be believed. Sloan's
diaries are informal and rapid, but they always retain the
respectful "Mr. Yeats," and Brooks proudly remembers
sitting "at the feet of the grand old Yeats." In a situation
where the cult of youth was pervasive, JBY managed to
be a friend to the young without losing his dignity, and a
believable sage without losing his wit, or his honesty.
He had the good sense, too, not to become a parody of
himself. When asked by an Englishwoman to play an old
shepherd in a sentimental Christmas play called "Eager
Heart," he promptly refused, following Quinn's advice:
"Tell her to go to hell!"

In New York—at Petitpas, at Sloan's, at one gallery
or gathering or another—his career as a conversationalist
was fulfilled and his reputation solidified. Lily wrote to
Quinn that her father "was born the year of the big wind,
1839," and the busy recipient of so many letters and
listener to so much talk must have been amused. But his
audience seems never to have begrudged his volubility
or tired of his endless *tremulo* in the vo' e, Padriac
Colum said, that "never went flat or ordinai y. His love
of conversation and pride in his own was partly experi-
ential and partly national. He liked good talk enough
to be descriptive and analytic about it, and one of his
earliest and one of his latest essays cover the subject.
Americans do not talk well because they are idea-ridden,
over-serious, and socially ill-at-ease; the English are
clever but mean; the Irish, less purposeful and more
poetical, indifferent to commerce and progress, cultivate
"a bright mentality functioning freely" and the dis-
course that follows. Good conversation requires intel-

lectual vigilance, social courage, and a real subject—but not an ideology or a doctrine. It also needs sympathy and caution: "A good talker is like a mariner entering strange, uncharted seas, who will drop his plummet again and again and make his soundings." Conversation is the social side of art, at once gestation, creation, and criticism: "Talk is man's sowing-time, and as he sows, so shall he reap. Literature is the harvest of talk."

JBY's topics—the substance of his conversation and correspondence and essays—were as endless as his energy: Irish politicians and writers; American food and women; British privateness, French gaiety, and German efficiency; aristocratic meanness and democratic restlessness; the psychology of creation and adaptation; the claims of art and the nurture of human personality. His was an elusive mind, eclectic and unsystematic, independent rather than original, humane, widely sympathetic, and altogether unspecialized. Ezra Pound once complained that both JBY and WBY had minds "a bit wooly at the edges" and that JBY's letters, once he realized they were to be published, became explanatory and journalistic. He does have the amateur philosopher's delight in Large Questions, and he is sometimes comfortable with his own understandings to the point of blandness, or cliché, or both. The unprofessional eagerness may be dangerous, but it is also brave and appealing. JBY is committed to an adequate though casual response to life. He once proposed "that the word invitation should be substituted for temptation since we really came on earth to be tempted, and that in most cases it was our business not to resist but to yield to it and take the consequences, even tho' it required the courage of a hero." He cherishes the concrete as the final test of both art and morality and the essential agent of whatever unity he can discover between them. If JBY has any one, dominant measure of achievement, of excellence and excitement, it is "the wild spirit of . . . imagination wedded to concrete fact . . . poetry in closest and most intimate union with the positive realities and complexities of life."

That measure is not a standard capable of systematic elaboration; and, while he occasionally worried about inconsistency, he never made consistency a positive virtue. He was not so sure about Emerson's effect on the American intellect, but he agreed about hobgoblins and little minds. One of his earliest essays claims that people paint because of wayward impulses and a gifted eye, and that formal education is likely to spoil their talent. He praises "an amicable unphilosophic frame of mind," insists that genuine happiness is growth not order, and is sure that "it is better to be illogical than INHUMAN." But amicability and waywardness are not timidity or dishonesty, and JBY is perfectly capable of an occasional tough assertiveness. He recognized that it is sometimes necessary not to be a gentleman; he attacked the "curtain of deceit" in Ireland during the *Playboy* controversy; he refused to see Kuno Meyer, who had tried to create Irish support for Germany during World War I and had blandly dismissed the sinking of the *Lusitania;* and he was severe, even bitter, when he found his son personally indifferent or politically authoritarian.

JBY is a hard man to "place" philosophically, and it is often difficult to get hold of his intellectual bearings, but there are some clear points of definition. An acute obituary writer for *The Freeman* said:

The truth is that he was at bottom an old-fashioned Anglo-Irish country gentleman, redolent of the classics, a sceptic of the eighteenth-century tradition, or of the tradition of Erasmus and Montaigne, who had also drunk in his youth at the spring of "political economy" and John Stuart Mill; and upon this foundation had been superadded, to the confusion of the simple, the doctrines of Rossetti in painting, of Morris in economics and of Irish Nationalism in the political sphere. It was a combination that made for an infinite, if somewhat bewildering, wit—a wit, however, that, where spirits were concerned, drew the line just the other side of the banshee.

That sounds right, except that "tradition" is too firm a word; his nationalism was more Georgian than modern, and he was more deeply and permanently affected by early nineteenth-century literary ideals than by their later variants. He is more of a genuine romantic than aesthete, symbolist, or pre-Raphaelite. His numerous representations of the poet more often than not return to the bold humanism of Wordsworth's *Preface:* "Art for Art's sake is for those who hate life, as many poets do, or who hate ideas, as again many poets do. The great artist is also a man like unto ourselves, and great personality is the material out of which is woven all his Art."

His sense of the motives and character of poetry finds its most natural kinship with Keats. In *Reveries over Childhood and Youth,* WBY recalls that his father did not read "that most beautiful poetry which has come in modern times from the influence of painting." That is almost certainly a misremembering, as JBY's correspondence, from the beginning, contains allusions and praise; and it is clear that he returned to the letters and poems with

enthusiasm: "Lately I have been reading Keats: he is so
young that you can read all his thoughts—he is so transparent—his purpose was against every discouragement
to find the truth." He discovered a temperament and a
set of allegiances, for all the differences in historical
moment and age and situation, encouragingly like his
own. There is, first of all, the emphasis upon the concrete,
the perceived connections between pleasure and pain,
the overwhelming sense of desire. There is Keats's
famous empathy and vitality, which JBY called "the
poet's seriousness . . . his quest for . . . the poetic omnis-
cience; a continual progress in identifying himself with
everything that lives, and that does not live, not merely
men and women or animals and birds but even trees and
plants and rocks and stones." There is the same relative
indifference to religion (which JBY recognized and en-
dorsed in Keats) in favor of artistic needs and "the
perennial human vivacity—as ancient as the sea. We are
told it makes the angels weep; it certainly causes the
moralists and the saints to scold a great deal. To artists
and poets and men of imagination it is perennial nourish-
ment and a joy." There is a similar conviction that lesser
imaginations admire while the capable imagination
loves: "The real thing is to understand, and love that
you may understand; that enriches the blood and feeds
it upon poetry. . . . When people really understand they
don't admire, and they can't quarrel. An affectionate
mother never admires her children, she knows them too
well, and she knows them because she loves them."

   That distinction comes close to one of the central distinctions in Keats's letters; he calls it, in the now famous
phrase, *Negative Capability,* "that is when a man is capable

of being in uncertainties, mysteries, doubts, without any irritable reaching after fact and reason," the belief that the strong imagination "lives in gusto, be it foul or fair, high or low, rich or poor, mean or elevated—It has as much delight in conceiving an Iago as an Imogen." JBY shares that determination and has had his own sharpened and strengthened by reading Keats. His desire and his language are similar when he writes to his son that his "only philosophy" depends upon "the consciousness of mortal ignorance" coupled with a conviction that the large and lucky imagination will discover vitality *and* harmony. Like Keats complaining about Wordsworth or coaching Shelley, JBY is suspicious of the tryanny of idea and will, and urges instead a sort of poetic passivity, an ability to receive without stern judgment. One of the things he most admired about John Sloan, and wished to nurture in him, was what he called Sloan's "won't power," his determination to be more artist than teacher, propagandist, or journalist. With JBY as with Keats, there is also an edge of despair about the imagination's capabilities: "Grand majestic spirits will spurn it, but passive, inactive beings like myself, and all of us when the time comes that energy can no longer help and pride is humbled, will return to it as a last hope, and as indeed the only hope left."

He is also, of course, the child of his age, struggling to survive its skepticism, its sense of loss, its pestering awareness of limitation and circumscription. His politics, in most healthy ways, do return to Mill, and his idea of criticism (not art) is more or less Arnoldian ("to criticize is to neither praise or denounce, but to *get nearer your subject"*). He shares the nineteenth century's empiricism and rationalism, its discovery of psychology and preoccupation with personal growth. While the life of the artist and the nature of art do organize most of his thoughts, there is an admirable, scratching, utilitarian corner of his mind that cannot forget quotidian human suffering. He wrote to Oliver Elton that "the world will not be right till poetry is pronounced to be life itself, our life being but its shadow and poor imitation"; but unlike the *symboliste* heroes of his son's generation, he quickly added that such a world will only exist "when science and intensive agriculture and intensive production and perhaps birth-control shall have obtained such a hold on things that poverty shall be as far away as the black plague of the middle ages."

If his ideas about art are most characteristically Romantic, about politics Utilitarian, and about criticism Arnoldian, his social and cultural sense remains Georgian Anglo-Irish—and that is probably because Anglo-Irish culture was created by the eighteenth century and rather limps along during the nineteenth, moribund but surviving, like his own estates. In temperamental bias and social instinct, he is urbane, skeptical, and conservative. In *Recollections of Butler* he celebrates the "orthodox inertia . . . characteristic of artists. They do not go to church, they never give a thought to religion, but they are profoundly orthodox in a deep, untroubled somnolency." He is suspicious of movements and fashions, schemes and reforms, recognizes the lesser arts—like courtesy and gossip—that hold a community together, and appreciates the amateur: the country gentleman or parson, the idle reader, the minor writer. He has a highly developed sense of style in talk or work or manner, and an affection for the slow pace of an established, organized society. He enjoys sentiment and satire (Goldsmith and Swift) and the sense of location and ethos that make both possible. His recollections and celebrations of eighteenth-century Anglo-Ireland are less historical than mythic: they define social arrangements and human relationships that he admires and, very occasionally, discovers or achieves.

It is the old-fashioned gentleman in him that accounts for the curious fact that a man who stood in a fatherly relationship to so much modern art distrusts modernism. He is always capable of particular judgments on individual works, but is inclined to find any movement faddish, doctrinaire, or strident. He does not like the restless experimentation he finds in New York and resists abstract art, though he does come to a qualified admiration for impressionism and its vital, sketch-like quality that leaves much to the imagination. He prefers representation over technique, meaning over expression, and attacks free verse—"Is it not another attempt on the part of democracy to make poetry as clamorous and common as itself." He is not fond of realism or naturalism or the literature of disenchantment—"Ezra's Poets are like the dogs that licked the sores of Lazarus." His conservative instincts, real love for the old literature, and sense of an ordered community make him, like so many men caught between "late Victorian" and "early modern," a man appealing to a tradition that he cannot quite pin down. It is to his credit that such a situation never made him reactionary, and only rarely cranky.

The "Life and Opinions" of JBY form a series of

shifting, acute responses and valiant contradictions. The ready conversationalist and gregarious companion, pleased with and known in three countries for his "joyous amiability," writes moving letters about his loneliness. He also develops a theory that the "superior man," especially the serious artist, is necessarily solitary: "*Art is solitary man,* the man as he is behind the innermost, the utmost veils," or "*A man is most intense when alone.*" He does not mean "living alone," nor does he mean anything as current as "alienation." New York was a very mitigated exile, and he had little use for silence or cunning. What he does mean (at least most of the time) is the self-reliant imagination—an idealized combination of integrity, instinct, and receptivity that he sometimes calls "the artistic doctrine of sincerity." It is an idea that goes back to his love for his father, his uneasy respect for the Pollexfens, and unqualified admiration of Isaac Butt, is shaped by friendship with people like York Powell, and sharpened by his sense of the lives of his favorite authors. It is part of his romanticism, and it stays with him all his life: "Poetry is the voice of the solitary, as resonant and pure and lonely as the song of the lark at sunrise. If the lark were to bother itself about the 'Collective Soul' of the Universe, it would not sing at all."

"Character," WBY wrote to his father, "is the ash of personality"—and JBY was delighted. The "splendid sentence" demonstrates, in a most gratifying way, the sympathy with which his notions were being received. "Character" he associates with abstraction and logic, uplift and will and nerves, action and power, the English and their Success, the Professionals and their

Bureaucracy ("as interesting as Berlin governed by its police"). Character is the malign triumph of Puritanism and of Commerce: "In thought I have always seen the Puritan minister sitting in company with the Father of the Family in a sort of horrid conspiracy to poison life at its sources." The essential qualities of Personality are spontaneity, vitality, and abundance; it reaches for harmony and wholeness, self-expansion and self-fulfillment; it values imagination, play, and instinct; it is the achievement of the Irish with their transformation of failure, and of gentlemen and artists with their sense of uniqueness and continuity.

The theory or description of Personality—or "human nature when undergoing a passion for self-expression"— is tied to his ideas about art and the artist. JBY is not advocating occasional or exclusively personal art, however, about which he has both romantic and conservative reservations. When the intense personality enters "into the world of art," he writes, "the personal ego is dropped away." The artistic personality at its fullest reach no longer needs the ego's assertiveness; in its tenderness and self-reliance it is like "the strange self-love of the hero when he is abandoned by his followers. . . . forced back upon himself he must still love." Man creates art out of a whole personality, but art also creates its own personality, and nourishes it in others. "I am sometimes asked," he wrote in *Early Memories,* "what it is that artists & poets aim at.

> I answer, it is the birth, the growth, and expansion of ever-living personalities. That is the value or the charm of a picture or poem. I read a poem or I look at a picture; these, if they be works of art, embody a personality. A personality

is a man brought into unity by a mood, not a static unity, (that is character) but alive and glowing like a star, all in harmony with himself. Conscience at peace yet vigilant; spiritual and sensual desires at one; all of them in intense movement. In contact with such picture or poem, the mood enters into my mind, pervading soul and body, so that for the moment I become a living personality, with, for dominant note, joy or sorrow, or hope or love. . . . Naked we come into the world, and naked we should remain if we retain personality and have the wizard's spell.

Man makes art, and psychology becomes aesthetics; but his equation works both ways: a man in the presence of art is enlarged and fulfilled. JBY is happily circular, and his contradictions, while never altogether resolved, are muted and made manageable by his steady determination to refer everything to a loose and capacious understanding of Mind. He has a genuine, philosophical interest in "the psychological question of the nature of belief" and thought, and he begins with a common-sense distinction: logicians and other men of character deal in theory, opinion, and argument—which leads to conviction; poets and personalities depend upon intuition and experience, habit and desire—which leads to belief. Occasionally the words "conviction" and "belief" get interchanged in his exposition, but he holds to the basic distinction. Sometimes he argues that ideas are merely the machinery of poetry, that Blake, for example, is serious about his system only in his prose: "the substance of his poetry is himself, revolting and desiring." But he is attracted to ideas, likes to talk about them, claims a "reverence" for them, and suggests Keats again when he insists that "poetry and the imaginative life can only flourish where truth is of supreme moment." He suspects the tyranny of the practical, abstraction and rationalistic explanation, but he admires curiosity, working things through, and strenuous, empirical thought. There is, he argues, a Herbert Spencer in every great poet.

JBY is most clearly endorsing a familiar nineteenth-century notion that ideas in art must be dramatic rather than dogmatic, that belief and truth must be absorbed into imaginative experience (most typically as "longing" or "desire"), that doctrinaire art is bad art. "Both philosophy and poetry," he maintains, "come out of the heart of belief," but it is belief as experience, not diagram. The qualities engendered in a mind as it encounters ideas are as important to him as the ideas themselves; his reflections on T. W. Rolleston provide some characteristic terms:

> Why is T. W. R. so disappointing? He is artistic, intellectual, a born litterateur—but he has no *desires,* that is to say no imagination. When you express to him some joyous, swelling idea—he produces some foot rule made by the University or the Department and *made on **wrong** principles.* In fact he has a donnish and bureaucratic mind.

He believes that "a poet must be, before everything, a servant of truth," and he likes to see that service as a kind of domestic relationship: "It is only in the unrestrained familiar conversation of truth, naked and unashamed, that the poet can draw easy breath. He must, as it were, walk affectionately, with her arm through his—then he can write poetry in which will be the heartbeat and the warm breath and the fragrance of her

presence." He adds, a touch uneasily, "am I growing
too dithyrambic?" and such a vision of the happy marriage of art and truth does have its problems. It is fine
for Art to be comfortable with Truth, but comfort is
likely to limit the particular truths that a particular
artist is willing or able to face and explore. JBY does
rather generalize his own moments of relaxed optimism; he is able to see adversity and tension lurking
around his perceptions and metaphors, but he wants
to see them resolved: "Belief & affection are the two
forces that inspire and control the poetical mind. The
energy of their ceaseless conflict is the energy of the
poetical mind and their reconciliation and union is the
militant triumph of the poetical mind."

In his aesthetics, as in his politics and his psychology,
JBY most often begins with an idea about the nature
of art or the place of the artist. So he sometimes sounds
(and has been seen) as if were a late-nineteenth-
century, art-for-art's-sake subjective idealist:

> Only for his dreams is a man responsible—his actions are
> what he must do. Actions are a bastard race to which a man
> has not given his full paternity.

> The tangible is valuable only for the sake of the intangible.

> The esthetical is the basis of society.

> The chief thing to know and never forget is that art is
> dreamland and that the moment a poet meddles with ethics
> and the moral uplift or thinking scientifically, he leaves
> dreamland, loses all his music and ceases to be a poet.

> To find out what was the mind of Shakespeare is valuable,

but the real thing is to find out what is my own mind when I read Shakespeare or any other poem.

Yet he has too acute a sense of the concrete and the contingent for those ideas to be sustained. Even when he celebrates the dream, actuality and temporality worm their way into his observations. After rereading *David Copperfield,* he writes Susan Mitchell: "That book is all a dream; everything in it is taking place in an impossible world—made out of *desire*"; but he immediately adds "and if there is any of the actual world—and there is much—it is only because desire has to build its dreams out of the only materials to its hand." He is willing to accept "art-for-art's-sake," but shrewdly argues that what the slogan usually means is technique-for-technique's sake, or manner-for-manner's-sake, and that he rejects, just as he rejects Academy painting and precious verse. He proposes instead "a new doctrine which I will call the doctrine of the *enviroment,*" a reaction to life but not an escape, an encounter with "reality, minute and particular and flushed with life."

JBY is simply too sociable, too tolerant and generous, and too optimistic to maintain an esoteric or hermetic view of art. He admires and urges upon his son a "democratic art . . . which unites a whole audience" and approves of the practical as well as the fine arts. He begins one letter, "my theory is that we are always dreaming," and concludes it: "These artists who say that representation of the fact hinders art are sinning against the first law of art—for *art is imitation*—and art is concrete, because you can only imitate concrete things." The apparent contradiction between expressive and mimetic assumptions about art is really a casual and hopeful dialectic: "Sleep is dreaming away from the facts and wakefulness is dreaming in close contact with the facts, and *since facts excite our dreams and feed them we get as close as possible to the facts if we have the cunning and the genius of poignant feeling.*" JBY did dream a lot, recorded his dreams as well as he could, and took them seriously. So "dreaming" is not exactly a metaphor; but it does operate in his thought as a kind of diminished version of Coleridge's secondary imagination—that human quality that is in touch with the concrete but transforms it, that can mediate between the quotidian and the transcendent.

In less lofty moods he seems to concede everything to life, only to immediately claim it again for art. The letter about *David Copperfield* continues: "The world is vanity saith the Preacher—it isn't. God made it, it is reality, and art and poetry are vanity; that is, they have no existence outside man's imagination—and what is not this kind of vanity, is neither poetry nor art or humour or anything else that is important. By logic and reason we die hourly; by imagination we live." A "realistic" skepticism gives way to ironic assertion, and another sentence, written about the same time, flatly claims that "poetry is the only reality, everything else is change and chimera." That sounds a bit ninetyish and does accurately reflect one predisposition. When his argument has a social or political implication, however, he is likely to use "poetry" and "reality" with an Orwellian rather than a Paterian purpose. In an essay for *The Independent* he argues that "Ireland is to be rescued neither by Belfast nor by England, neither by priest nor by parson, but by its artists," because only they could provide "freedom of thought and the intoxication of truth . . . an unshackled intellect." His last essay, "The Soul of Dublin," makes a similar point. He liked (and needed) to remind his son of the inherent conflict between poetry and power: "Napoleon hated Literary men" because he and others like him "cannot afford to see facts in their reality: the fact for instance, that millions of men were being butchered in his wars, for a phantom glory." The poet can and must and, if he is honest, does. For a man of his age and generation, usually bored with practical politics, living out his life in a city where he could not vote, JBY remained impressively alive to the subversive powers of art.

So he is, amidst all the shifts and contradictions of his responsiveness, fundamentally an old-fashioned humanist and romantic optimist. He does believe that "all poetry is woven out of humanity," does insist on that "union with the positive realities and complexities of life," and that art is an intensified representation of life. All his central predilections support that view: the doctrine of personality, the claims for portraiture, the love of conversation and correspondence with their particular sense of audience, the desire to achieve unity out of diversity, to conjoin the order, peace, and beauty of art with the intensity, plurality, and uniqueness of life. Like the great Romantics, he insists on the interplay between the artistic imagination and the concrete, perceived object. Art is imitation, he holds, with a wealth of suggestion and love, a transforming attention to detail passionately beheld, a meeting of the world and "the dictates of a kindled imagination." That view is reflected in his admiration for Sloan (genius *and* historian), his attraction to literary biography, his wish to discover and define the artist as hero. His favorite authors—Shakespeare, Goethe, Dickens, Tolstoy, Keats—are those whom he feels to be most fully in touch with life. His least favorite are the mannered ("Swinburne is the poet of surely the thinnest humanity ever known") or the rarefied ("I have just read a long novel by Henry James. Much of it made me think of the priest condemned for a long space to confess nuns"). In the middle of World War I he wrote a long letter to Oliver Elton that is impressive and characteristic in its recognition and acceptance of current reality and its brave assertion of higher claims for the imagination's response to life:

> Soldiers though they be heroes are wise according to the wisdom of others, and so it is with the loud multitude for whom the rhetoricians labour in their vocation. The poets remain the protesting voice for the other wisdom, the true wisdom, that of human nature, which would get out of its cave of false honour—and real dishonor and defeat;—seeking the liberty to be itself, so that every intuition and instinct might bear blossom and fruit.

It is a body of thought more derivative than original, more responsive than creative, more casual than systematic. The life of John Butler Yeats was brilliant and fruitful, but it was not so much a monument to intellect as it was a triumph of personality. He was a man who not only survived his burdens, but defeated them; who could, in spite of loneliness and anxiety and frustration, write to Oliver Elton, "I look forward confidently to a millennium," and to his son (in a letter approaching his seventy-seventh birthday and preoccupied with "senectus and old Father Time") that "there is always with me a residuum . . . a conviction, an intuition inseparable from life—that nothing is ever really lost." His last essay (perhaps his last writing of any kind), "The Soul of Dublin," appeared in *The Freeman*, without editorial comment, twelve days after his death. It is self-consciously valedictory and rehearses the old themes: the celebration of Irish idleness, conversation, and art; the gentle mockery of commerce, materialism, and unionism. It reaffirms his Anglo-Irishry without rancor and with considerable valor. The last letters poignantly reveal a sense of his own death and of the fact that he will not go home: "The desire to go on living is the passion and sin of the old man and the scorn of the young. . . . In youth we do not see death, the stage is too crowded. In old age all the actors have left—and they were only actors—, and death remains sitting patient on its stool." Yet he can misquote *Hamlet* convincingly:

I have always believed that we are always upon earth, I also believe there is a providence

Rough hew them how we will
there is a providence that shapes our ends.

I have no belief in what is called a personal God, but I do believe in a shaping providence—and that this providence is what may be called goodness or love, and that death is only a change in a world where change is a law of existence.

And he can conclude a letter six months before his death (a letter to his son, which begins "I have been an unconscionable burden" and which reasserts the value of his self-portrait) with the authentic voice of Edgar, after his, his king's, and his father's holocaust: "Ripeness is all."

There are few lives that more successfully and movingly embody what Erik Erikson has called the final stage of the life cycle, or "integrity": "It is the ego's accrued assurance of its proclivity for order and meaning—an emotional integration faithful to the image-bearers of the past and ready to take, and eventually to renounce, leadership in the present. . . . It is a sense of comradeship with men and women of distant times and of different pursuits who have created orders and objects and sayings conveying human dignity and love." Shortly after Ann Butler Yeats was born, JBY wrote to Elizabeth that he "would like to see Willie playing with his own child. From the first, whenever American people came up to me in the American way and shouted: 'How you must be interested in your grandchild,' I replied 'No, not a bit, but very much so in seeing my son as father.' Is it because I shall never see her grown up?" Such health and generosity of spirit is a great gift, and one that the poet did not—could not—fully understand until many years later, well after his father's death and close to his own. In *Last Poems*, full of reverence and recapitulation, JBY has become an image, mythic, a leading member of all that heroic company of WBY's breath-taking career. His personality—as being and as doctrine—has *become* his son's utterance, an emblem of domestic concern, artistic integrity, Anglo-Irish pride, and other beautiful, lofty things:

My father upon the Abbey stage, before him a raging crowd:
'This land of saints,' and then as the applause died out,
'Of plaster saints': his beautiful mischievous head thrown back.

There is another filial tribute, less famous perhaps, and tacit, but very right. Jack B. Yeats was reticent about both his father and his work, but he admired JBY and, in one of his few discussions of his career, said flatly and several times that he painted because he was the son of a painter. One of his last paintings is a huge canvas called "Glory," done in 1953, four years before his death. It is powerful and triumphant and vivid, and it depicts three figures—son, father, grandfather—meeting together and greeting the glory of a western Irish landscape and of their own existence. The painting celebrates generational continuity and expansive life. The old man—thin, athletic, one hand exuberantly waving his cap, the other holding aloft the golden-haired, shouting boy—recalls the indestructible Bowsie of Jack's novel, *The Charmed Life*. It also bears a family resemblance to the grand progenitor of the astonishing Yeatses.

Selected Bibliography

I. PRIMARY SOURCES:

A. Books by John Butler Yeats:

Essays Irish and American. Dublin: Talbot; New York: Macmillan, 1918.
Early Memories: Some Chapters of Autobiography. Churchtown, Dundrum: Cuala Press, 1923.

B. Fugitive Essays and Reviews:

"The Royal Hibernian Academy and Home Rule in Art." *The Sanachie* 2 (1907): 1–9.
"The Rationale of Art." *The Sanachie* 2 (1907): 113–26. Reprinted as "Watts and the Method of Art" in *Essays Irish and American.*
"Can Americans Talk?" *Harper's Weekly* 53 (March 6, 1909): 11–12.
"The Difference Between Us: An Irish Spot-Light on Some English and American Contrasts." *Harper's Weekly* 53 (December 11, 1909): 24–25.
"The American Girl: An Irish View." *Harper's Weekly* 54 (April 23, 1910): 12–13.
"Why the Englishman is Happy: An Irishman's Notes on the Saxon Temperament." *Harper's Weekly* 54 (August 13, 1910): 10–11. Reprinted in *Essays Irish and American.*

"Outdoors in New York: An Irishman's Impressions of the Spirit and Temper of the Metropolis." *Harper's Weekly* 54 (November 19, 1910): 11–12.

"Brutus' Wife: An Irishman's Views of the Woman Suffrage Question." *Haper's Weekly* 54 (January 14, 1911), 14–15.

"Back to the Home: An Irishman's Reflections on Domestic Problems and Ideals." *Harper's Weekly* 55 (April 29, 1911): 12–13. Reprinted in *Essays Irish and American*.

"Synge and the Irish: Random Reflections on a Much-discussed Dramatist from the Standpoint of a Fellow-Countryman." *Harper's Weekly* 55 (November 25, 1911): 17. Reprinted in *Essays Irish and American*.

"The Modern Woman: Reflections on a New and Interesting Type." *Harper's Weekly* 55 (December 16, 1911): 24–25. Reprinted in *Essays Irish and American*.

"Ireland to be Saved by Intellect." *The Independent* (New York) 72 (January 25, 1912): 191–94.

"Our Cousins Overseas: Some British Traits as Seen from the Viewpoint of a Celtic Painter." *Harper's Weekly* 57 (February 15, 1913): 11–12.

"A Painter on Painting." *The Seven Arts* (April, 1917), pp. 677–80.

"John Sloan's Exhibition." *The Seven Arts* (June, 1917), pp. 257–59.

"Recollections of Samuel Butler." *The Seven Arts* (August, 1917), pp. 493–501. Reprinted in *Essays Irish and American*.

"The Work of John Sloan." *Harper's Weekly* 58 (November 22, 1917): 20–21.

"J. B. Yeats on James Joyce" [Essay-letter to John Quinn, October 14, 1920], edited by D. T. Torchiana and Glenn O'Malley. *Tri-Quarterly* 1 (Fall 1964): 70–76.

"Talk and Talkers." *The North American Review* 213 (1921): 527–38.

"A Painter of Pictures." *The Freeman* (New York) 4 (January 4, 1922): 401–2.

"The Soul of Dublin." *The Freeman* (New York) 4 (February 15, 1922): 541.

C. Correspondence:

Passages from the Letters of John Butler Yeats. Selected by Ezra
  Pound. Churchtown, Dundrum: The Cuala Press, 1917.
Further Letters of John Butler Yeats. Selected by Lennox Robin-
  son. Churchtown, Dundrum: The Cuala Press, 1920.
J. B. Yeats: Letters to his Son W. B. Yeats and Others, 1869–1922.
  Edited with a memoir by Joseph Hone. London: Faber
  and Faber, 1944; New York: E. P. Dutton, 1946.
"John Butler Yeats to Lady Gregory: New Letters." Edited
  by Glenn O'Malley and D. T. Torchiana. *The Massachu-
  setts Review* 5 (Winter 1964): 269–77.

II. SECONDARY SOURCES:

Archibald, Douglas N. "Father and Son: J. B. and W. B.
  Yeats." *The Massachusetts Review* (Summer 1974).
Brooks, Van Wyck. *John Sloan: A Painter's Life*. New York:
  E. P. Dutton, 1955.
———. *An Autobiography*. New York: E. P. Dutton, 1965.
Ellmann, Richard. *Yeats: The Man and the Masks*. New York:
  Macmillan, 1948.
Hone, Joseph. *W. B. Yeats 1865–1939*. New York: Macmillan,
  1943, 1962.
———. "Memoir of John Butler Yeats" in *J. B. Yeats: Letters
  to his Son W. B. Yeats and Others, 1869–1922*. London: Faber
  and Faber, 1944; New York: E. P. Dutton, 1946.
Jeffares, A. Norman. *W. B. Yeats: Man and Poet*. London: Rout-
  ledge and Kegan Paul, 1949, 1962.
———. "John Butler Yeats," In *Excited Reverie: A Centenary
  Tribute to William Butler Yeats, 1865–1939*. Edited by A. Norman Jeffares and K. G. W. Cross. New York: Macmillan,
  1965.
Murphy, William M. "Father and Son: The Early Education
  of William Butler Yeats." *Review of English Literature* 8
  (1967): 75–96.
———. "In Memory of Alfred Pollexfen': W. B. Yeats and

the Theme of Family." *Irish University Review* 1 (1970): 31–47.

———. "The Ancestry of William Butler Yeats." *Yeats Studies* 1 (1971): 1–19.

———. *The Yeats Family and the Pollexfens of Sligo.* Dublin: Dolmen Press, 1972.

Pyle, Hilary. *Jack B. Yeats: A Biography.* London: Routledge and Kegan Paul, 1970.

Sloan, John. *John Sloan's New York Scene: From the Diaries, Notes and Correspondence, 1906–1913.* Edited by Bruce St. John. New York: Harper and Row, 1965.

Reid, B. L. *The Man from New York: John Quinn and his Friends.* New York: Oxford, 1968.

Yeats, William Butler. *Autobiographies.* London: Macmillan, 1955, 1961.

———. *The Letters of W. B. Yeats.* Edited by Allan Wade. London: Rupert Hart-Davis, 1954.